CW01335827

RUINS

Their Preservation and Display

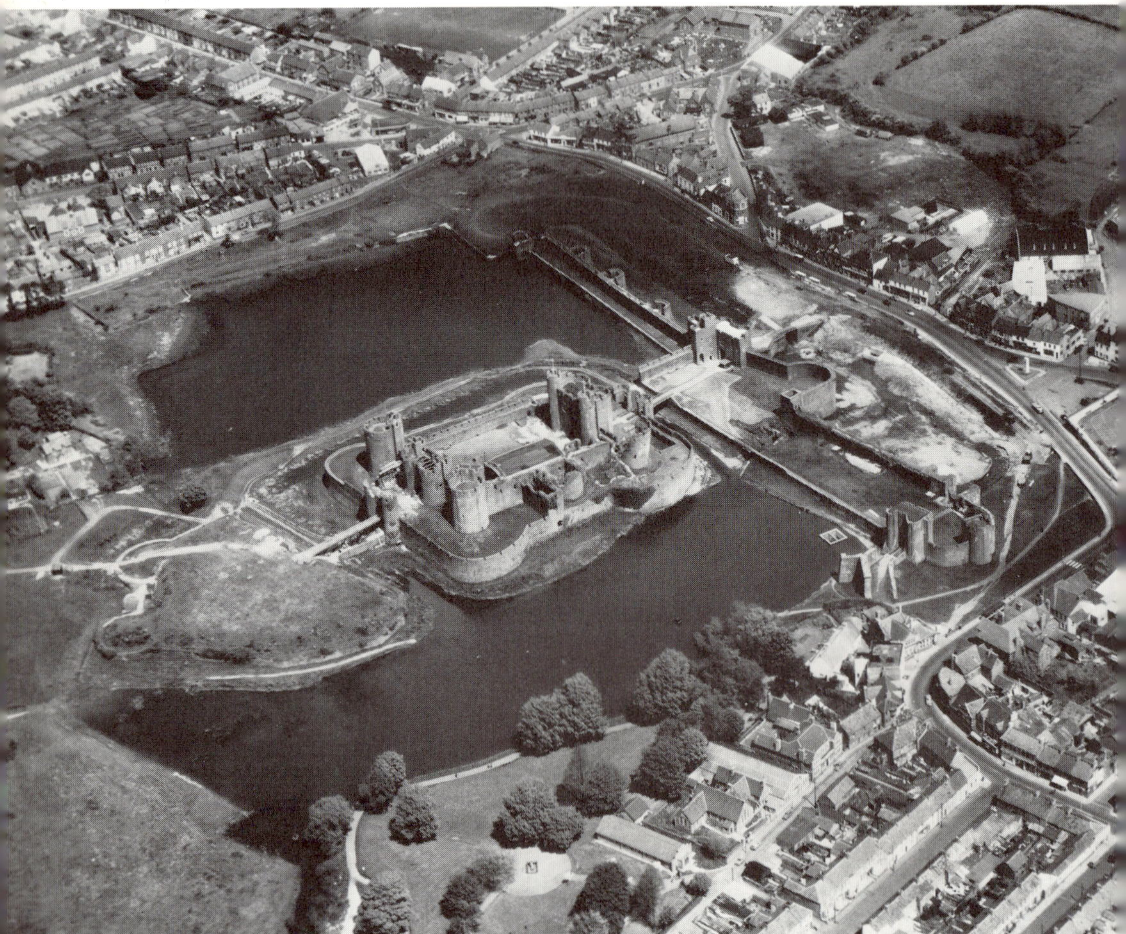

RUINS

*Their Preservation and Display
M. W. Thompson*

A Colonnade Book
Published by British Museum Publications Limited

Colonnade Books
are published by British Museum Publications Ltd and are offered as contributions to the enjoyment, study and understanding of art, archaeology and history.

The same publishers also produce the official publications of the British Museum.

Frontispiece: aerial view from the south-west of the castle and lakes at Caerphilly, Glamorgan.

© 1981 M. W. Thompson

Published by British Museum Publications Ltd,
46 Bloomsbury Street, London WC1B 3QQ

British Library Cataloguing in Publication Data
Thompson, Michael Welman
   Ruins.
   1. Historic buildings – Great Britain –
   Conservation and restoration
   I. Title
   720'.941   NA109.G7

ISBN 0-7141-8034-3

Set in Monotype Bembo by S. H. Elder Ltd,
Beverley, North Humberside
and printed in Great Britain by
Pindar Print Limited, Scarborough, North Yorkshire

Contents

Acknowledgments	6
Preface	7
Introduction	9

PART I
1	Growth of Interest	13
2	Preservation	22
3	Display	29

PART II
4	Retrieval	35
5	Restoration	57
6	Representation	71
7	Access	77
8	Interpretation	85

Conclusion	95
List of Works Referred to in Abbreviated Form	98
Notes	98
Index	101

Acknowledgments

Grateful acknowledgment is made to the following for permission to reproduce plans and photographs:

Aerofilms Ltd: 3, 9, 33, 34, 37, 52; Cambridge University Air Photographic Collection: frontispiece, 6, 17, 18, 19, 20, 21, 22, 23; Department of the Environment (Crown Copyright): 7, 10, 11, 12, 13, 16, 26, 27, 36, 39, 45, 46, 48, 53; J. Lingwood: 28, 41; M. Murray: 38; Royal Commission on Ancient and Historical Monuments in Wales (Crown Copyright): 29; P. Scott: 24, 25; C. Smith: 40; Mrs A. E. Thompson: 8, 35, 42, 43, 47; Welsh Office (Crown Copyright): 2, 4, 5, 14, 15, 30, 31, 32, 49, 50, 51; West Air Photography: 44.

The quotation on p. 13 is made with the permission of the Council of the Early English Text Society, and the figure on p. 93 and quotation on p. 94 are used with the permission of the Society for Medieval Archaeology.

Preface

When I came to Cardiff a little while ago, few things impressed themselves more on my mind than the great contrast between, on the one hand, the massive restoration of ruins undertaken at the castle and Castell Coch by William Burges for the Marquis of Bute and, on the other, the preservation of existing remains, as they stand, by the Government service concerned with these matters. It was clearly a subject for exploration and explanation, although it became plain at an early stage that the first step was to understand the treatment of ruins as it has been carried out over the last seventy years. There is no general study, no periodical to which one can turn for an account of this work, and indeed much of it has now passed beyond living memory.

The result has been this essay—I use the word advisedly—which is an attempt to give an account of the treatment of ruins without straying into the architect's sphere on one side nor into the official aspects of it on the other. As the Notes at the end of the book disclose, it has had, inevitably, to be drawn largely from my own experience. The choice of terms may be unfamiliar to some who work in this field, but I hope they are valid descriptions of what is being done. In the future they will no doubt be superseded by definitive terms in an authoritative textbook.

The word textbook makes one recoil, the more so as the work is directed as much, or indeed more, to the general reader as to colleagues in this and cognate fields, such as museums. The considerable jargon that the subject generates—architectural, antiquarian, legal and Civil Service—has been curbed to a minimum, although one cannot dispense with it altogether. For example, the portmanteau legal term 'ancient monument' which so confuses different concepts and is so alien to everyday speech is deliberately avoided. The relatively short length of the book will also, perhaps, be an encouragement to the prospective reader.

It is a particularly pleasant task to acknowledge my debts to others, especially colleagues, whether architects or Inspectors, from whom over the years I have learnt so much. The only name that it would be right to mention specifically is the now-retired Assistant Chief Inspector of Ancient Monuments, Mr R. Gilyard-Beer, who for many years was my mentor in this matter. His lectures at Rome, York and elsewhere had gone some way to create a rationale of ruins. The debt will indeed be recognised, although paternity for the errors should not be laid at the same door.

Finally, it should be emphasised that nothing in this book should be construed as representing the views of the Welsh Office or any other Government department, nor can anything that is said here be regarded in any sense as Government policy.

M. W. Thompson
Cardiff, 1981

Introduction

Most houseowners are aware of the unrelenting struggle against decay: painting, cleaning gutters, replacing tiles and so on. Although deterioration begins as soon as the house is erected, it accelerates with age, and a point may be reached where the contest is given up. Once water can penetrate the structure, the wooden floors and roof will rapidly rot until the house becomes unsafe and unfit to live in. It can then be said to be derelict, but as the timbers fall in from roof and floors it can be described as a roofless ruin. The same result will of course be produced much more rapidly by fire. It is this roofless shell to which the name ruin is applied throughout this book. The shell may stand to roof height or exist only as a foundation (or even merely as an archaeological fossil in the subsoil), but it is clearly sharply distinguished from a roofed structure which provides shelter and is in some sense usable.

Historic ruins in Britain are the subject of this essay, but before we turn our backs on those abroad, it would be useful to survey a wider field to compare the causes of survival of ruins in different parts of the world[1]. We shall then see the matter in a less parochial light.

It is perhaps a moot point whether natural erosion or human interference is the major agent of destruction. Fire and pillage may create ruins, but deliberate levelling and quarrying for the reuse of stone or brick are probably their main enemies. The denser the population, the more likelihood there is of interference, and similarly it follows that the sparser the population the less the interference with ruins in the area. It is no accident that the main monastic ruins in Britain occur in rural as opposed to urban situations, and that the most impressive ruins are to be found as often in the tropical forests of Indo-China and Central America as in the barren deserts of North Africa and the Middle East.

The other agents of destruction are the natural effects of climate and vegetation, the two being closely related. The ceaseless wear of rain on mortar and stone, the action of frost, the activity of roots in loosening the masonry (thus allowing frost greater action) need no lengthy description. In fact, it is probably a combination of wide seasonal variations in temperature with high precipitation that is the most potent factor. There are no frosts in the tropical forests of Indo-China, and while there may be sharp daily variations in temperature in the desert or severe seasonal fluctuations in, say, Asia Minor, the rainfall is much less (and so too the consequent vegetation) than in temperate or northern Europe.

The third factor to be weighed is the varying degree of resistance of the passive materials of which the ruins have been constructed to withstand these destructive forces. We are told of Samarkand: '. . . the mosques and tombs and colleges and minarets waste slowly like corpses and will one day sink into the desert'.[2] It is indeed well known that unbaked, or imperfectly baked, brick cannot withstand the weather, and similarly Devonshire cob will melt into the ground unless it is covered on top. Until a few centuries ago the principal building material in temperate or northern Europe was wood, but wood does not form ruins. One may see derelict timber-framed houses in various parts of the country, but it would be a matter of surprise to see the roofless ruin of a timber-framed building anywhere. No stone or brick has a permanent life, but their durability is very variable; chalk or clunch unless rendered over will have a very short life, but a good magnesian limestone should have great endurance. Most stone will last indefinitely indoors under cover, but even apparently hard stone, like Purbeck marble or alabaster, will crystallise or decay quite quickly in the open air.

From this brief survey it is clear that conditions in the British Isles are more or less at their most hostile to the survival of ruins. Since the Industrial Revolution the population density has been one of the highest in the world; the climate and vegetation are entirely inimical to ruins; the traditional building material until Tudor times, timber, is too perishable to form ruins at all. Yet in spite of this, or perhaps because of it, ruins in this country are probably more solicitously cared for and elaborately displayed than anywhere else in the world. Why and how this is so is the subject of this essay.

Of the three factors mentioned one only can be controlled by legislation: human interference can be prevented, or at all events severely curtailed, by prohibitory laws. Since the main Act in 1913[3] some 20,000 monuments, predominantly ruins or earthworks, have been protected, that is, added to the statutory list ('scheduled') in England, Scotland and Wales. Difficulties of enforcement make it impossible to prevent all human interference, but the law has certainly slowed it down sharply.

Laws cannot prevent erosion and collapses caused by climate and vegetation, and these continue to affect most ruins. The same legislation has, however, allowed the state to play a more positive role in preservation in a limited number of exceptionally important cases by taking the remains into care. There are some 800 or 900 monuments, predominantly ruins, in the care of the state, and it is with this activity that this book is concerned.

However much solicitude may be lavished on a ruin, it has no indefinite life; we can take steps to prevent it falling down, but we cannot prevent erosion of the stone by the weather. The removal of decorated stone crosses from out of doors into a church, the only ultimate solution for saving the carving, is a tacit admission of what applies to the larger (and usually later) medieval ruins. It is quite likely that the removal of the protective layer of fallen debris at the base of a ruin hastens the erosion of the dressed stone and thereby shortens the life of what must in any case have a finite life. Here we are touching upon a fundamental point that during this finite life we are making use of the ruin by rendering it intelligible to the visitor, both for pleasure and instruction.

The scale of the Government's activity in the care of monuments is not always grasped. In 1977 some seventeen million visitors were attracted to monuments (largely ruins) in custody in Britain (obviously there is no record of the number of visitors to monuments which have no custodial staff). The enormous growth in numbers of visitors in recent years is no doubt closely related to the great increase in privately owned motor cars in the period since the Second World War, of which more will be said later.

It is not the purpose of this essay to deal with the organisation for preserving ruins in Britain, but as it may be quite unfamiliar to readers it cannot be entirely ignored. Since the first legislation in 1882, the care of ancient remains has been regarded by the Government as a works function, settled on the Office of Works and its descendants, currently the Department of the Environment (the Scottish and Welsh sections were devolved to their respective national departments in 1978). The day-to-day management of the monuments is in the hands of architects, advised by Inspectors of Ancient Monuments. A distinctive feature of the British system is the large body of directly and permanently employed industrial staff organised under their regional superintendents. These consist of craftsmen (masons and carpenters) and labourers who work in small groups of three to twelve on the individual monuments scattered up and down the country. It is this permanent labour force which gives continuity and uniformity to the British system; had it been decided from the start to do all the work by contract, a much more heterogeneous organisation and treatment of the remains would certainly have resulted.

It was felt at the time of the 1913 legislation that it would be an unwarranted intrusion into the rights of private property to bring inhabited buildings under the provisions of the Act and accordingly they were excluded. Only since the war have measures been introduced in planning legislation to protect inhabited buildings. The curious result has been that the distinction between ruins and used buildings that I made earlier has virtually the force of law. Furthermore, although the Government gives grants of money to historic buildings, it plays no part in their physical preservation, so that the works organisation that I have just described is devoted very largely to the preservation of ruins. Indeed, the organisation might be regarded as a body of specialists in ruins, the only ones in the country.

A ruin normally passes into state care under deed of guardianship, the owner retaining the freehold but the cost of maintenance and management becoming the responsibility of the state. A careful assessment of the architectural and historical importance of the structure, together with the cost of preservation works, is made before the ruin is accepted. As a ruin is a liability to the owner, there is normally no shortage of candidates for adoption by the state.

When a ruin comes into care, it may have suffered from centuries of neglect and may indeed be in a state of collapse. There is first a period of retrieval works carried out by a small gang and lasting five, ten or twenty years, according to need and the size of the monument. When the retrieval has been completed, it is then largely a question of routine maintenance, although the initial treatment may have to be repeated in thirty or forty years.

This essay is largely concerned with the operations of retrieval which may be on a much larger scale than is often appreciated. Indeed, the expression 'tidying-up' that I have heard used is hardly appropriate for the employment of a light railway! In no two cases is the work the same, but I hope that there are sufficient common principles to make the book worth while.

It is often asked whether this portion of a ruin has been rebuilt, or what it is proposed to do about that section, and so on. In Part I I set out the principles that govern the treatment which has been reached over a long period of time during which people have held varied views as to how ruins should be used; so we have to start off with history. In this controversial subject we have to a great extent learnt by the mistakes of our predecessors as our successors will no doubt learn by ours. The nature of preservation, the actual treatment of masonry, as well as other aspects of retrieval, are then discussed, and the first part concludes with some observations on the complicated issues of display.

The extraordinary difficulty of trying to categorise the work carried out on ruins is perhaps the main reason why no one has attempted before to deal with this subject. In Part II I have frankly relied on the illustrations to make the points, and it is not claimed that the chapters represent an exhaustive division of the work carried out on ruins; it is the before-and-after appearances which are amenable to photography that have been largely used here. In some cases the scale of the operation was so great that it almost deserved a volume of its own, but obviously in this small work it was out of the question to devote unbalanced space to it. Again, the examples used are highly selective, depending on my knowledge, or lack of it, and the availability of photographs. Through ignorance I have had to confine myself to that with which I was familiar. Medieval ruins are the central subject, but it has been felt necessary also to pay some attention to prehistoric and Roman remains, different as the problems are in those cases. Industrial ruins have been excluded.

The satisfaction and pleasure of writing an essay of this kind is to understand one's own actions in a field which is still largely innocent of explanation in spite of the enormous labours in it over the last sixty years.

PART I

1 Growth of Interest

So long as there are stone buildings there will be ruins, and we may reasonably regard ruins in Britain as traceable back to 4000 BC or earlier. The communal tombs constructed of huge undressed blocks in the neolithic period, although not always conforming to our definition of a ruin (where the capstone survives), have yet to be regarded as such for the purposes of preservation. More consonant with the definition are the bases of circular and rectangular huts found in the highland areas of the west, or even the earlier enigmatic stone circles. The great hillforts may, indeed, also in some sense be regarded as ruins, particularly where the defences consisted of stone walling. While we must not ignore these early works, yet it remains true that ruins in Britain were created on a large scale by political events at two periods in history: the end of Roman Britain as a province of the Roman Empire in the fifth century AD, and the events associated with the Reformation in the sixteenth and seventeenth centuries, more especially the Dissolution of the Monasteries and the Civil War.

The Ordnance Survey map of Roman Britain might lead one to expect that extensive remains would be visible, but disappointment awaits the traveller with this expectation. Remains of town or fort walls exist at Lincoln, Colchester, York and elsewhere, but otherwise most of what we see has had to be laboriously dug out of the ground. Even Hadrian's Wall can be a disappointment on the first visit, so much lower does the masonry stand than expected. To see impressive Roman remains we must go south to the Mediterranean area, for while it is doubtless true that the structures erected in Roman times were more impressive in north Africa than in Britain yet their very unequal survival is eloquent testimony to the greater strength of those forces of destruction in Britain mentioned in the Introduction (see p. 9). The Roman ruins in Britain made a much deeper impression on the Anglo-Saxons who saw them at a date much closer to their erection, as this translation of the well-known Early English poem, probably referring to Bath, shows:

> Splendid is the masonry – the fates destroyed it
> the strong buildings crashed, the work of giants moulders away
> the roofs have fallen, the towers are in ruins,
> the barred gate is broken. There is frost on the lime,
> the gaping roofs are shattered and decayed,
> and sapped by old age. The clutch of the grave
> the strong grip of the earth, holds the master builders . . .[1]

Roman remains in Britain have reached us, then, mainly in an archaeological aspect, but the medieval antiquities to which we now turn constitute genuine ruins and are indeed the most prominent antiquities in the non-industrial landscape. By far the greater part of Government expenditure on preservation is directed to these remains, for in the eyes of both specialist and non-specialist the state is regarded—with some justification—as primarily concerned with preserving abbeys and castles.

The termination of the monastic way of life in England and Wales took place in a very abrupt manner. The Acts of 1536 and 1539 dissolved the religious houses, and within a year or two they had been divested of everything of value. One of the most valuable materials was the lead on the roofs of their churches, the stripping and melting down of which gave rise to the most dramatic creation of ruins in English history. The multitude of chantry colleges founded in the later Middle Ages were dissolved in the reign of Edward VI. It was a veritable orgy of ruin-making.

The consequences of the Dissolution and the ruins it produced were profound, affecting English thinking for the next four centuries[2] and indeed right up to the present day. For the first century after the catastrophe the ruins had too close a relationship to current events to allow the existence of a detached view. Ruins are very evocative emotionally as we know, for example, from the burnt-out mansions caused by the troubles in Ireland or the Revolution in Russia, and they may recall even distant events (particularly in Celtic countries). Monasteries have Popish overtones for Methodists, and castles in Wales an aroma of Edward I! It was only in the middle or late seventeenth century that a more detached attitude could reveal itself, a feeling that prompted the classic collection of monastic records published by Sir William Dugdale in *Monasticon Anglicanum* (1655–73). As Aubrey wrote: ' . . . the eie and mind is no less affected with stately ruines than they would have been standing and entire. They breed in genrous minds a kind of pittie; and sett the thoughts a works to make out their magnificience as they were when in perfection.'[3]

Another class of ruin created more indirectly by the Reformation must be mentioned—castles, abandoned completely after the Civil War. There are no figures available, but the total is probably to be counted in hundreds. From innumerable surveys of Tudor and Stuart times it is known that a great many castles were already derelict, but instead of fading away like old soldiers they were reactivated, usually by a Royalist garrison, during the Civil War, and after capture by Parliamentary forces rendered unusable or 'slighted' to deny them to the enemy. At the Restoration a great number of these stricken castles were abandoned.

Monasteries were usually placed on low-lying sites, but castles were built on hilltops, so the latter type of ruin is a much more conspicuous feature of the landscape, particularly in Wales or the March where the number of abandoned castles is very great. On the other hand, the much finer detail and the regularity and intelligibility of the monastic plan following that of the parent order on the Continent have attracted the modern student. Until the late Professor Hamilton-Thompson in the early years of this century showed that there was an intelligible development in the plan of castles they were regarded as haphazard structures, not to be compared to monasteries. In Government preservation abbeys have been regarded, certainly up to the Second World War and probably since, as the monuments *par excellence*, most worthy of attention.

Religious attitudes towards ruins were greatly eased by the intrusion of the eighteenth-century belief in nature, giving God a place off-stage as it were. In the contemplation of nature there was solace to be derived from a ruin:

> While, ever and anon, there falls
> Huge heaps of heavy moulder'd walls.
> Yet Time has seen, that lifts the low,
> And level lays the lofty brow,
> Has seen this broken pile compleat
> Big with vanity of state:
> But transient is the smile of Fate!
> A little rule, a little sway,
> A sunbeam on a winter's day
> Is all the proud and mighty have
> Between the cradle and the grave.[4]

Dyer looking down from Grongar hill into the Towey valley in 1727 reminds us of Wordsworth looking down into the Wye valley at the end of the century.

Dyer later went to Rome and wrote a poem on its ruins. The interest in Classical ruins for both picturesque and archaeological reasons goes back earlier to the seventeenth century, but by the middle of the eighteenth century native Gothic ruins had become something of a cult. We cannot pursue this delightful subject in all its ramifications, although we must mention the prints of the first half of the eighteenth century. Samuel Buck, assisted usually by his brother Nathaniel, has left us over 400 prints, showing very largely ruins, which with all their imperfections represent more often than not the first visual record of many ruins now in state care (1).

It is important to remember that there was no question of preservation in the Romantic or Picturesque attitude towards a ruin. The ruin was there to stimulate and excite the onlooker; whatever increased the theatrical effect—ivy or moonlight—was desirable to heighten the sensation. William Gilpin in his journey down the Wye in 1770 said of Tintern:

> 'More picturesque it certainly would have been if the area, unadorned, had been left with its rough fragments scattered round; and bold was the hand that removed them; yet as the outside of the ruin, which is the chief object of picturesque curiosity, is still left in all its wild and native rudeness; we excuse—perhaps we approve—the neatness that is introduced within.'[5]

He described in considerable detail the vegetation growing on the abbey which in his view enhanced it.

Lest it be thought that Gilpin was eccentric in his views, Arthur Young, the agricultural improver, visited Fountains Abbey at about the same time and found clearance going on of which he disapproved.[6] The circumstance caused him to enter into some detail on 'the just stile for a ruin to appear in. We generally find them in retired, neglected spots, half-filled with rubbish, and the habitation rather of bats, owls, and wild beasts, than of man: This horrible wildness greatly strengthens the idea raised by falling walls, ruined columns and imperfect arches; both are awful, and impress upon the mind a kind of religious melancholy...'

Gilpin had suggested using a mallet to improve the silhouette of Tintern Abbey, and there is no doubt that many ruins suffered from selective demolition where the remains were not visible from the house or in a vista. The pleasure could as well be derived from an artificial ruin, a folly, as a real one. The ruin became like a toy in the landowner's park.

1 Caerphilly Castle, Glamorgan: view of the east side by the Buck brothers, 1740.

The strange folly on the hill at Shobdon, Herefordshire, known as Shobdon Arches, shocks modern susceptibilities since we still see the Middle Ages through the lens of the Gothic Revival. In the middle of the eighteenth century the medieval parish church at Shobdon had been pulled down, except for the tower, and rebuilt with a most attractive 'Gothick' interior. The highly decorated Norman chancel arch was set up on a hill overlooking the church, the doorways slightly behind it linked by the tympana. The remains have suffered severely from erosion which has obliterated the carving on one tympanum. The erection of this eighteenth-century folly constructed from genuine twelfth-century remains was regarded as praiseworthy at that time, although it repels us now. For the Enlightenment the attitude towards medieval remains was definitely *de haut en bas*, and only with the dawn of Romanticism was there a feeling of sympathy. Sir Richard Colt Hoare on his annual visits to Wales grieved at the deterioration in the west end of the church at Llanthony Priory between 1793 and 1803.[7]

The question of Romantic or non-Romantic attitude occupies so central a position in the discussion of ruins that we are bound to pursue the subject a little further. Even the most down-to-earth person can feel his imagination stirred by a ruin, and that is of course his main source of pleasure and satisfaction. Edward Gibbon, it will be recalled, was prompted to write *The Decline and Fall of the Roman Empire* by reflections one evening among the ruins on the Capitoline Hill at Rome with the sound of friars chanting in the background.

If there are other conditions, such as moonlight or thick vegetation, then the imagination produces quite a different state of mind. I recall a visit to the nineteenth-century, neo-Gothic Bayon's Manor, Lincolnshire, when it was derelict but before it was demolished. The dripping from leaves over this 'castle' produced a most eerie experience. Similarly, on another occasion at Carcassonne in France during a bitterly cold February day the wind banging the shutters of Viollet-le-Duc's restoration created an uncanny sensation. This was the sort of feeling that the eighteenth-century visitor tried to induce in himself from a ruin.

The pleasure of a ruin is to stimulate our imagination and reconstruct in our mind's eye the structure in its original state. The better we understand the ruin (common sense or, if necessary, archaeology), the better the imaginative reconstruction. If it requires ivy and moonlight or the occasional fall of a stone to stimulate excitement, then this is probably a form of self-dramatisation and a different, more theatrical, experience. The boundary between the two is blurred, and the Romantic tends to flit from one side to another.

Let us now turn to the Gothic Revival, that curiously and peculiarly English phenomenon arising from an infusion of piety into the Romantic experience.[8] The whole story of Victorian restoration that occupied the middle decades of the nineteenth-century is far too long to relate here, but we must have some knowledge of it if only to understand the reaction that followed.

Nineteenth-century restoration is criticised less severely now than it was a few years ago, but its results still shock us. There can be no doubt that many churches, if not derelict, were certainly in urgent need of repair and extensive restoration. The strain of piety in the restorer's attitude towards Gothic architecture led to an almost

17

unbalanced belief in its virtues, for as Gilbert Scott said: '... I boldly assert, that no style of architecture which the world has ever produced has shown a tittle of this elasticity in adapting itself to every circumstance, position and material.'[9] There is no doubt that restoration required a much deeper understanding of Gothic architecture, and it is no accident that two of the greatest students of the subject were amongst the greatest restorers, Gilbert Scott and Viollet-le-Duc.

Viollet-le-Duc under the heading 'Restauration' in volume viii of his great dictionary of Gothic architecture declared that a new art had been born in the second quarter of the nineteenth century—scientific restoration. Scott was much more coy, and it is indeed a little difficult to reconcile the account in his autobiography of what he did with his lectures at the Royal Academy to his students on what ought to be done. His own poem may be quoted (the last two lines of which refer precisely to what he was later criticised for by William Morris):

> Beware lest one worn feature ye efface,
> Seek not to add one touch of modern grace;
> Handle with reverence each crumbling stone,
> Respect the very lichen o'er it grown:
> And bid each ancient monument to stand
> Supported e'en as with a filial hand,
> 'Mid all the light a happier day has brought
> We work not yet as our forefathers wrought.'[10]

Probably the most uninhibited restoration carried out in Britain in the style of Viollet-le-Duc was that by William Burges for the third Marquis of Bute at Castell Coch, a few miles north of Cardiff. The architect's report to his patron together with water-coloured pen-and-ink plans and sections survive,[11] so we know the thinking behind the work. These plans were made in 1872 after the clearance of the moat and interior of the castle, a work on a scale comparable to those carried out by the Government in recent years. There were no hasty decisions, and the rebuilding which began in 1875 had not been completed at the death of Burges in 1881. The ruin upon which the new structure was erected was decidedly fragmentary; the ground-plan and basements are medieval, but the superstructure is conjectural (2). The exterior is a more or less faithful reconstruction after the principles of Viollet-le-Duc, but the interior is fantasy. Nevertheless, by its boldness it is undoubtedly a considerable architectural achievement, comparable on a much smaller scale to Carcassonne (3). The original thirteenth-century castle that inspired it was probably a drab affair beside the reconstruction, a little bit of the Rhineland introduced into Wales!

The reaction against 'the fatal practice of "restoration", which in a period of forty years has done more damage to our ancient buildings than the preceding three centuries of revolutionary violence, sordid greed (utilitarianism so called) and pedantic contempt'[12] is of course associated with William Morris and the Society for the Protection of Ancient Buildings (founded in 1877). It is not the purpose of this essay to follow this reaction, but some understanding of it is so closely bound up with the later treatment of ruins by the state that we cannot appreciate the motives of the latter without some understanding of the former.

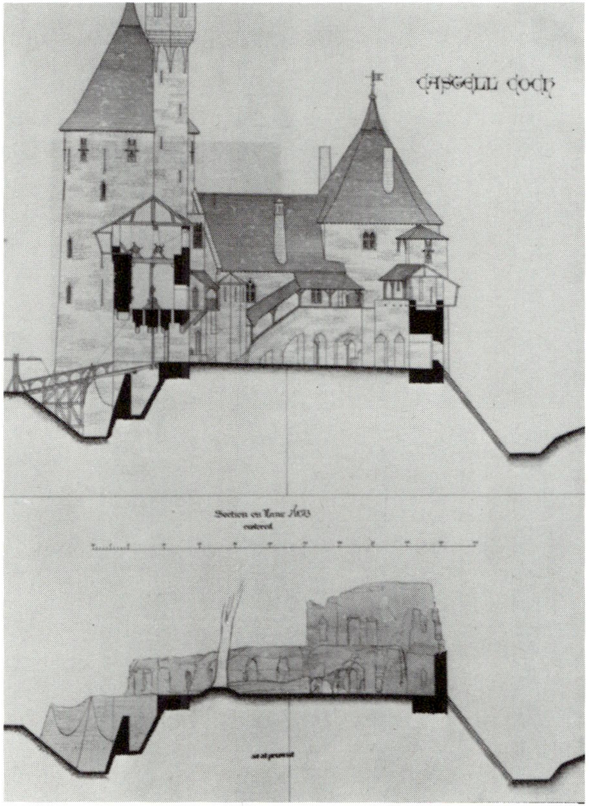

3 Castell Coch, Glamorgan: aerial view of the castle as it is today.

2 Castell Coch, Glamorgan: section by William Burges through the ruin showing what was proposed and what existed in 1872.

Morris claimed to be a disciple of Ruskin:

> '... what Ruskin then taught us was simple enough ... that the art of any epoch must of necessity be the expression of its social life, and that the social life of the Middle Ages allowed the workman freedom of individual expression, which on the other hand our social life forbids him.'[13]

Morris, then, had ideals that grew from the Gothic Revival. It was not a religious view, that neo-Gothic architecture was an expression of a religious revival, but a sociological or political attitude derived from an idealised form of medieval society which was the source of his admiration for the Middle Ages. This led him to (or perhaps derived from) a condemnation of modern society and so to a socialism with which many of his contemporaries did not sympathise. By the end of the century, however, his views on preservation were widespread among architects, that owing to changed social conditions it was not possible to restore faithfully and even if it were it would be undesirable.

The description by Morris of Sir Gilbert Scott's restoration of the chapter house at Westminster Abbey neatly defines the point:

> 'He "carefully restored" the Chapter House, that is, he made it (we are speaking of the exterior now) a modern building, imitating with as much success as is possible in such cases the work of the thirteenth century. It has no longer any claim to be considered as a work of art; it is the architect's architecture, the work of the office, in which the executants are in no degree taken into council.'[14]

After the death of Morris the Society for the Protection of Ancient Buildings continued. We may quote their austere remarks from the *Notes on the Repairs of Ancient Buildings* of 1903:

> 'The conditions and surroundings of every period are different, so that the motives which act on men of one age cannot govern the productions of genuine work conceived in the spirit and embodied in the forms of another ... Even were it possible to reproduce lost work, it may be said that in matters artistic honesty is the best policy, just as much as in other affairs of life. The restorer is in reality committing a forgery, and if he succeeds in deceiving ...'[15]

Honesty and truthfulness are words that we will hear bandied about on the ruins today, but the word which is missing and to which we shall return is 'evidence'.

Two years later in 1905 G. Baldwin Brown took a similar view in his book advocating new legislation for the protection of ancient monuments.[16] The Royal Commissions to investigate historical monuments were set up in 1908, a new Inspector appointed in 1910 (after a lapse of ten years) and the basic legislation enacted in 1913. The Society's rigorous views were adopted by the state service concerned with preservation from the start and have remained with them ever since. In the Inspector's Report for 1913[17] restoration was regarded as the most heinous offence making a foreman liable to 'instant dismissal'. It remains at the core of all thinking on this subject.

The dominant factor in the minds of those concerned with preserving ruins today is an awareness of the value of the remains as evidence. The ruin is regarded as a document which can tell us a great deal about its history if we have eyes to see and understand. The remains may be fragmentary, but from slight traces, such as a springer here indicating a vault or there a window, a picture can be formed in the mind's eye of the original building. It will be appreciated at once that the preservation is that much more informative if this kind of evidence is kept and wherever possible left exposed for the discerning eye to see.

A structure in use rarely remains entirely unaltered; there are countless reasons for enlarging, reducing, rebuilding and so on. Medieval (and of course Roman and prehistoric) buildings underwent repeated changes in several centuries of use, for which their ruins contain evidence; without some grasp of the changes that took place during the active life of the structure it is almost impossible to understand what one is looking at (see pp. 85-8).

The father of 'structural archaeology', as study of these changes is called, was Professor Reverend Robert Willis (1800-75), whose correlations of written with architectural evidence at Christ Church Cathedral, Canterbury, and later at the colleges of Cambridge University laid the foundations of the subject. In the early years of this century there was a brilliant flowering of this school associated particularly with the name of Sir William St John Hope. The period saw the invention of dated plans showing periods of construction indicated by colouring or shading, which later became such an essential feature of official guidebooks (see p. 31). The creation of the state service for preserving ruins coincided with this flowering of structural archaeology which has become very much a permanent part of its thinking. The early exponents had been particularly interested in the recovery of the full plan of monastic ruins where the much higher degree of decoration and elaboration of the ecclesiastical architecture made dating much easier than on secular sites. In 1910 Charles Peers, one of the practitioners of structural archaeology became Inspector (later Chief Inspector) of Ancient Monuments and thereafter laid down the basis of state treatment and display of ruins.

The first monuments to come into care under the 1882 Act were mainly neolithic chambered tombs. The Inspector then appointed was General Pitt-Rivers, an archaeologist,[18] which meant that the organisation started off with an archaeological bias. Peers was a trained architect, but his successors have been archaeologists. The whole unwritten assumption behind the British system is that an architect and an inspector work together, the former looking after the practicalities, the latter providing the criteria and historical knowledge to give direction to the work.

Finally, a question that is often asked is why ruins in Britain are regarded as a works and not a fine art matter, as they are on the Continent. When private legislation was proposed in the 1870s, it was indeed intended that they should be looked after by an independent commission. The Crown already had a number of castles in its care, and at the dis-establishment of the Irish church in 1869 a large number of ecclesiastical ruins were transferred to the Board of Works in Dublin; the logic of the situation was clear when new legislation was to be introduced. The craftsmen and labourers required for preservation are the same as those used in the building trade. A works organisation, like a contractor's business, is no doubt fairly insensitive, but preservation on the scaffolding in all weathers is inevitably a fairly crude and insensitive matter. The disadvantages are outweighed by the gains, the chief one undoubtedly being the continuity provided by a permanent labour force.

2 Preservation

Why cannot a ruin be simply left alone to preserve itself? After all, the great majority of ruins in this country are left to their own devices, so why does the state undertake 'preservation' on a small minority of the most important ones?

Some remains, such as earthworks or megaliths or stone circles, are undoubtedly best left alone. A descriptive notice may be erected, a fence put round the remains to keep the cattle off, and that appears to be the end of the matter. But what date is to be put on the notice? Normally the remains will be dated by analogy with similar remains elsewhere, but it would be much more satisfactory to find pottery of known date in the ruin, or better still charcoal for a radiocarbon date. If the stones of the original structure have collapsed in a meaningless heap, then surely it is desirable to re-erect them in as near to their original position as can be ascertained? Some remarkable restorations have been carried out by the state since the Second World War, notably on the trilithon at Stonehenge, but this and other restorations will be discussed in Chapter 5.

Consideration of these early monuments has demonstrated two basic aims for the preserver: to secure what remains and to render what he secures intelligible both to himself and to the onlooker that he is going to invite to the site. Intelligibility is the foundation of the whole operation of preservation and display.

Different problems arise with the Iron Age and Roman period. Earthworks like hillforts are best left undisturbed, although in one of the excavations by the late Sir Mortimer Wheeler at Stanwick, Yorkshire, a short section of ditch was cleared and a length of revetment wall reconstructed as an experiment (see p. 64). Huts built of dry-stone walling, often circular, such as occur in Cornwall, Anglesey and elsewhere, require excavation and laying-out if they are to be intelligible (see pp. 52-3).

In the case of upstanding Roman masonry the problems are analogous to those of medieval ruins. The main difficulty with Roman remains is to render them visible at all, since they have to be laboriously revealed by excavation and then reset so as to be capable of withstanding the weather. If there are tessellated pavements or painted plaster, which cannot resist the weather, the only method of preservation for display is to roof them over, a costly operation that may lead to a disappointing result. Just as with a decorated cross (see p. 10) that could be preserved only by being out of the open air, so similarly with a Roman villa a new building has to be erected around it since the remains themselves cannot be removed.

When we turn to the central theme of this essay, medieval ruins, the first question to cross our minds is: why interfere with them at all? If they are more evocative in their present condition, with clinging ivy, why not leave them alone? The vast majority of privately owned ruins are left untouched. Ruins are deteriorating all the

4 Llansteffan Castle, Dyfed: back of the gatehouse before treatment.

5 Llansteffan Castle, Dyfed: back of the gatehouse after treatment.

time, and it is on practical and economic grounds only possible to halt this deterioration in a minority of cases by direct intervention which cannot in any case stop the erosion of the stone. Both the preservation and the display of the masonry require it to be freed from later accretions and vegetable growth. Photographs of the back of the gatehouse at Llansteffan Castle before and after the removal of the ivy speak for themselves (4, 5).

The objectives of the work in preservation are to arrest decay and freeze the masonry—as it were—in the condition in which it was found, and secondly to remove any accretion of structures or fallen debris or growing vegetation that conceals the stonework and is a deterrent to its preservation or the understanding of its original construction. The base of the walls in any ruin is normally buried to a considerable depth in accumulated debris, the purpose of removing which is twofold: the masonry must be treated to its original base; secondly not only is a very substantial (and often better-preserved) part of the ruin invisible under the ground until it is removed, but also the ground-plan cannot be determined until this has been achieved.

A medieval wall which may be from 60 cm to 4.5 metres thick consists of two faces of coursed, rubble or dressed (sometimes squared to ashlar) stones acting like the bread of a sandwich for the rubble core that fills the space between. The binding matrix for both core and face was lime mortar: the loss of adhesion of the mortar or its complete disappearance is one of the main problems facing the preserver. The dressed facing stones have often proved attractive to local people for reuse and so have been removed leaving shapeless lumps of core upstanding, themselves often swathed in ivy or other growth. The latter will be weakening the joints and mortar and may by sheer weight be pulling the wall over.

The principle of treatment is to start from the top of the ruin, which means scaffolding it, and then to work down to the original ground surface. After removal of vegetation, the top of the wall is reset in lime mortar so as to form an impermeable capping that will prevent water percolating down into the thickness of the wall. The object of the work is to renew the adhesion of the mortar. The surface joints are therefore raked out all the way down and pointed with fresh mortar, either directly into the cavities or over cement that has been used for 'tamping' at the back of the joint. If the mortar has lost its adhesion in the interior core of the wall, then liquid cement can be poured or pumped into it to set as a solid mass. The 'grouting', as it is called, tends to form a very rigid wall and, although a traditional method of treatment, is somewhat out of favour at present.

The lime used in medieval building was made on the site as a part of the constructional work. Nowadays a lime mortar of five parts sand to one part lime with some cement is employed, the colour of the sand chosen being varied to match the shade of the original mortar.[1] The mortar is set back in the joint with a steel point and washed and roughened. There is considerable skill in pointing as the briefest comparison of pointing at a monument with that done by a contractor, usually in cement and often projecting or flush, at any village church will show.

If the wall of the ruin is fractured, the normal method of overcoming this is concrete beams (steel rods set in concrete) embedded in the core of the masonry so that they are invisible. They can be used across a fracture at one or several points ('stitching') or around the whole circuit at the top ('ring beam') to bind the structure together. If the wall is actually leaning, it would normally be left, perhaps with underpinning, unless there was danger of it toppling, in which case it would have to be taken down and rebuilt. There may be rare cases when the cost is justified of making a leaning wall vertical, but it is an expensive and laborious operation.

In practice the handling of a dangerous ruin is a skilled matter requiring experience of where to scaffold, to support and to take down parts, as well as the choice of the right sequence of work in order to minimise the danger. There are few really skilled masons who can do this kind of work, and the mason has to some extent to be chosen according to the demands on his skill the ruin will make.

To what extent is 'restoration' (Chapter 5) justified in normal preservation, as distinct from reconstruction of prehistoric structures or adjuncts of monuments like gardens? The general rule is that one only restores or reconstructs where it is structurally necessary. For example, a mullion may be so eroded by the wind as to have lost its strength, but if it supports tracery above, then it will have to be replaced by a freshly cut mullion. If there is any risk of the mouldings disappearing altogether, then the sooner it is done (while they are recognisable), the better. Freshly cut stone can be inscribed with a date, so that there is no doubt about its modern origin. The general principle remains, however, that under normal conditions dressed or moulded stone is allowed to have its life and is not replaced.

The term 'representation' has been chosen for replacement of a missing feature by an unmistakably modern substitute and will be illustrated in Chapter 6. The theory is that by using a modern substitute, such as concrete kerbing for a missing wall or recessed and rendered brickwork to fill a void in a wall, one does not beg the question of missing windows and doors. There may be structural reasons for its use, but more often than not it is required for rational display.

The removal of later accretions has to be carried out at the same time as the treatment of the masonry, the two forming inseparable parts of the same operation. There are two or three very distinct kinds of accretion that have to be considered: accumulations of debris or soil which are due to natural deposition or demolition or dumping; or reuse of the ruin for quite different purposes by insertion of a new structure; or earlier eighteenth- or nineteenth-century restoration.

At an abbey or castle the accumulated overburden over the last level of active use can vary from 30 cm to 6 metres. At Bolingbroke Castle, Lincolnshire where the masonry on the outside had been completely buried to a depth of 1.5–6 metres, hundreds of tons have had to be removed. Preliminary study by excavation is essential to control the work, the object of which is to remove the debris from above the floor or ground level of the last period of active use of the building. With an abbey that came to an abrupt end in 1540 this is fairly easy, but it may be much more difficult with a structure that underwent a long period of lingering decay before expiring. It is to be sharply distinguished from research excavation which breaks through the last period of use and penetrates earlier levels to establish the earlier history of the site. For example, in a monastery it may be desirable to locate an earlier apsidal end preceding the square end of the church. The objectives and methods are quite different in this case.

6 Bury St Edmunds Abbey, Suffolk: aerial view showing the treated eastern end and encumbered western end.

7 Bury St Edmunds Abbey, Suffolk: the crypt and crossing laid out for display.

By lowering the ground surface the walls of the ruin are heightened, and quite often the lower part will retain facing and detail that have been removed higher up. The results can be dramatic and produce something unrecognisably closer to the original than the shapeless ruin that was the starting-point. There may, of course, be discoveries of tile floors, doorways, staircases, cellars, crypts and so on. As the whole ground-plan of the building unfolds, the results can be very exciting, or sometimes very disappointing, as at Rufford Abbey, Nottinghamshire, where drains and wartime constructions had virtually destroyed the abbey foundations that lay in front of the later house.[2]

The increased understanding of a ruin arising from exposure of the ground-plan will allow much more intelligent preservation; for this reason and because it is necessary for display, fuller understanding of the ruin is a constant objective at all times. The main obstacles to this understanding are the frequent changes that the structure has undergone both as a living building when it served its original purpose (to be discussed in Chapter 8) and since then up to the present day. The decisions that will have to be taken on retention during preservation will be some of the most difficult and controversial to arise.

At first the issue seems simple enough; the object is to display an abbey or castle, and the visitor will be bewildered and confused by the remains of any later structure on the site which accordingly should be removed. With a static water tank, a wartime Nissen hut or a nineteenth-century pigsty there will be general agreement, but suppose it is an attractive eighteenth-century dovecote or a seventeenth-century gateway? Some later additions constitute monuments in their own right, but it is the borderline cases which give rise to controversy. The proposal which gave rise to lively debate some years ago, to remove the early nineteenth-century houses from the west front of the abbey at Bury St Edmunds (6) well illustrates the point. The vista of the great abbey that would have been opened up and the dramatic silhouettes, worthy of modern sculpture, that it would have created were not sufficient to outweigh support for retention of the houses. It neatly shows the difficulty of reconciling the two interests which are indeed incompatible.

Decisions on the retention or demolition of later additions call for a great deal of experience and weighing, on the one hand of the merits of the structure in its own right or as illustrating the later history of the site, and on the other, of the detraction from the original building by obscuring it and confusing the onlooker. Patterns of walls produced during alterations to the original foundation can be as complicated as a railway marshalling yard without the further confusion of the later remains of cattlesheds or garden walls. Some painful decisions will have to be made.

A particular case is earlier restoration. Sometimes this is very rough-and-ready estate work and can be fairly easily removed. Sometimes a kind of folly has been created and this again presents no problems. Far more difficult is the case of very extensive and expensive earlier restoration on the ruin as at Kenilworth or Caerphilly Castles (34). In such cases it is difficult to distinguish original from restoration, and there is little choice but to leave it, although its appearance is in conflict with the principle set out in this essay that what is displayed on the site are the authentic remains of the period to which they purport to belong.

This does not exhaust all the problems that will arise in the treatment of a ruin. One noteworthy omission is stone vaults that may survive over undercrofts, or even the main structure, in medieval ruins. The stones of the vault can be treated as a wall in so far as the mortar of the interstices is concerned, but the main object of the exercise is to prevent percolation of rainwater from above by laying a waterproof membrane on the top (extrados) of the vault. This skin can be protected by gravel if people are going to walk over it.

Other materials will be involved on the monuments: wood in roofs and floors, glass and lead in windows, iron in industrial monuments. This, however, takes us outside the field of ruins as defined at the beginning of this essay into the sphere of roofed buildings. It may be useful to contrast the nature of the work in the two distinct types of structure, since we are dealing with two different types of conservation, the confusion between which leads to endless misunderstanding.

There is perhaps an analogy between a ruin and an object in a museum: both are going to be displayed to the public, both come into custody requiring expensive conservation. Except in the case of an industrial monument or science museum where machinery is to function, the object of display is still and passive. No doubt it is very much easier to display an object indoors than a large structure at the mercy of the elements out in the open, but the principle is nevertheless the same in either case. With a roofed building an entirely new consideration is introduced: the parts must serve the function for which they were intended. In conserving an ancient roof the object is to preserve the maximum amount of the original timber, but the final result must be capable of bearing the load of lead, tile or slate that is to cover it. The floor that is to be treated must be able to support the weight of people walking on it, and the restored window must keep the wind and rain out. Compromises between renewal and leaving unaltered are therefore constantly required on a roofed building but are not necessary in a ruin. If the structure is to be brought into full use, many other considerations connected with services will also have to be taken into account. There is, indeed, no more fruitful source of confusion than that caused by the failure to distinguish between the objectives of those preserving a ruin and of those preserving used, or at all events, usable buildings.

3 Display

Chapter 2 was concluded with a comparison between an object displayed in a museum and a preserved ruin; it will be valuable to extend the comparison but this time to make it between the museum itself and the ruin.

A museum is an exhibition of objects having an origin at some distance from the building housing them, while a ruin is, of course *in situ*. Because of their small size museum objects are sought by collectors and command high prices, so that the auction rooms, from which much of the collection derives, play a large part in the ethos of a museum. Ruins cannot be collected and have only a high negative value, since to display them would cost thousands of pounds which cannot be recouped. The indoor work in laboratory or library at the museum produces a rather less hardy attitude than the wind and the rain on the scaffolding! The greatest contrast between the two is perhaps more apparent than real. The museum is by definition a seat of the Muses, a place for study, self-instruction and education; a monument, the legal term for a ruin, is on the other hand (*Denkmal* in German, *Pamyatnik* in Russian) a reminder of an event, person or activity.

The early legislators thought primarily in terms of preservation, intending that the monument should thereafter sufficiently remind the onlooker of the events that it recorded without further prompting. A large ruin is usually an extremely complicated structure, difficult to understand without the historical and comparative knowledge that the ordinary visitor lacks. The immense increase in numbers of visitors, due largely to private motoring, has greatly increased the demand for guidance, particularly as a great number of them come with no previous knowledge of medieval buildings. Furthermore, the great rise in expenditure on ruins requires a greater response to the needs and requirements of this influx. The general Civil Service term 'presentation', which covers the methods by which these needs are met, can best be rendered in everyday speech by 'display', the title of this chapter.

Display can be divided into two very distinct categories: requirements to satisfy the physical needs of the visitor and requirements to satisfy his intellectual needs. The first covers a wide range of matters from toilet facilities to bridges, while the second is largely, although not exclusively, a matter of publications. The sale of souvenirs has now become such a normal part of the service at privately owned historic houses that it is expected by the public, although whether it should be regarded as a physical or intellectual need may be a moot point!

Since ruins often survive in rural settings (see p. 9), it follows that the normal method of reaching them is by motor transport. Indeed, the widespread use of private motor cars or hired coaches has given many ruins a new lease of life! The provision of a car park at any important non-urban ruin in state care is now regarded as essential. The time spent in acquiring land for car parks in positions that will not detract from the monument is considerable, and equally with toilet facilities and sales points problems of concealment arise, which may require much ingenuity to overcome.

Wherever possible one tries to make the modern entry to a ruin correspond to the original one, in the hope that this will simulate the feeling of the original approach to the living building. Often conditions have so changed that this is not possible, but sometimes the original approach can be restored, with notable success, for instance, at Kenilworth Castle where it was possible to combine it with a new car park (see p. 80).

At the ruin itself the impression made upon the visitor by the masonry will be very much influenced by its surroundings. Flower-beds or anything that hints of a municipal park have always been frowned on (except in Scotland), no doubt because they would constitute a rival distraction from the ruin. A moment's reflection on the conditions of ruins in municipal parks will confirm the cogency of this argument. Where there were trees already growing by the ruins, these are usually retained and can considerably enhance its appearance. Trees growing on the masonry, however, have to be removed.

The whole ground surface of the ruin is normally closely mown grass, forming an extensive and well-tended lawn which can be a little bleak. Indeed, there is a tendency for the onlooker to be more impressed by the lawn than the ruin! Possibly this feature owes something to the cathedral close; the reasoning doubtless was that a ruined monastic church required the same reverence as a cathedral church in use. Furthermore, there is something of an English passion for closely mown lawns as evidence of tidy and efficient maintenance.

There are four considerable advantages to a mown lawn around a displayed ruin. First, the green of the grass and the grey of the stone are normally an aesthetically satisfying combination. Secondly, it allows the exposure of foundations or low footings or marking out in the grass where the original wall has been lost. Thirdly, it is generally dry and soft underfoot. Finally, but not least important, the maintenance costs are lower than any alternative.

One disadvantage of grass is that it cannot stand up to the heavy wear of a large number of visitors and has to be replaced from time to time. This has given rise to problems at Stonehenge, Fountains Abbey and elsewhere. Gravel can be introduced of course, either for paths or to contrast certain areas such as indoors as against outdoors in an open court.

The disappearance of the wooden parts of the ruin gives rise to a whole range of problems, both practical and intellectual. The former are mainly of access, particularly in castles and secular buildings. The disappearance of a bridge at a castle would leave the visitor confronted with a formidable moat or ditch; the wooden steps to a principal first floor have often disappeared; and the ascent of a tower may have required crossing at a certain level a now vanished floor.

In order not to restore on the one hand but not to erect an unsympathetic structure on the other the usual solution is the oak bridge with oak handrail that is such a conspicuous feature of castles in state care. It is designed to be unmistakably modern and to leave medieval features such as drawbridge pits exposed to view. Similarly, stairs and gangways are normally of oak. Concrete is very unsympathetic to stone, but its maintenance costs are much lower, while its tensile strength in ferro-concrete beams can allow unsupported spans far greater than timber allows (46). There is a tendency now to support wooden bridges on concrete beams partially concealed beneath the decking.

Those who work with ruins sometimes forget how bewildering a ruin can be for the ordinary person. The purely accidental shapes that have survived, the puzzling presence of face here but only core there, the complete absence of floors and roofs showing quite unfamiliar aspects of a building, the lack of plaster and exposure of harsh stonework; all these factors combine to present the ruin to the visitor in a somewhat brutal and enigmatic light. There are not the pictures, carpets and furniture of a historic house to wonder at, which was perhaps the main motive of the visit, but instead the rather bleak scene of a manicured ruin in a large expanse of lawn.

It must be recognised that not all visitors wish to make the concentrated effort that an appreciation of a ruin requires. Effort is indeed the right word, for even those who are very experienced in this field will find difficulty in understanding everything. The first step is to grasp sufficient of the ground-plan to identify one's position and thus orient oneself in relation to the other buildings. Monastic plans (except for Carthusian ones) follow a fairly regular pattern, the conventual buildings being subordinate to the church which, once recognised, allows identification of the other buildings. Castle plans are much less regular but much simpler, so that the identification of keep, hall and gatehouse allows one to determine one's position. The object of the plan in the official handbooks is to allow such orientation, and the lack of it in some historic houses open to the public is one of the main handicaps to understanding them. Plans can be displayed on boards, and the labelling of remains can be of great help.

The next step is to attempt in the mind's eye to restore to the fragmentary remains the roofs, floors and glazing of the original buildings. In a multi-storied building the absence of wooden floors helps one to see the stages all the way up, whereas the existence of a planked floor obscures everything above. Where the masonry is low, one is forced to a great extent to rely on analogy: a monastic church looked something like a medieval cathedral or parish church still in use; the surviving cloisters at Durham or Gloucester resemble the ruin; the surviving castle halls at Winchester or Oakham tell us something of vanished ones. Models or reconstruction drawings can help the imagination. At a great many ruins reconstruction drawings on postcards by the late Alan Sorrell are on sale.

The third and most difficult point to grasp is that structures serving living people are subject to repeated change and alteration. The building is too small or too large, is burnt down, is not grand enough, or is obsolete. The result is that the ruin as we see it today is the product of several major alterations during the four or five centuries that it was in use. Attempts to disentangle and distinguish these alterations are one of the main preoccupations of the person who writes the guide, and the plan he produces, in which the different kinds of shading represent the dates of the periods of construction, records the visible evidence for this. The abbey may have been founded in, say, 1140, but it is quite likely that there is nothing earlier than a hundred years later visible in the ruin: the twelfth-century church was swept away in the thirteenth; the abbot's quarters rebuilt in the fifteenth century; and so on. In his mental reconstruction of the monastery in use the visitor has to take into account and remember that it was not a constant, unchanging group of buildings.

For some medieval structures there is contemporary written evidence, notably records of building expenditure, that throw a great deal of light not only on when construction took place but how it was done. The main body of records to survive is that of the Crown so we are particularly well-informed about royal building operations.[1] We have, for instance, especially detailed information about the castle-building activities of Edward I during the conquest of north Wales, and this adds enormously to our appreciation and understanding of the great surviving ruins. Indeed, perhaps one of the most satisfying experiences to be gained from a ruin can derive from the close correlation with a written source and the greater understanding of its construction that this gives (see p. 87).

The general principles are the same whether the ruin belongs to a period without written sources, such as a prehistoric tomb, or to a period when there are no native written sources, such as a Roman villa, except that comparative material is the only aid in these cases. Broadly speaking, the greater the familiarity of the public with the subject, the easier they find the remains to understand: a castle is more intelligible than a monastery, since the assumptions behind monasticism are entirely alien to modern life. Consequently, the case for a museum and explanatory material is usually strong with the scanty remains surviving on, for instance, Roman sites.

The interpretative exhibition, derived from the national parks in the USA, has been introduced on a number of ruins in this country, with particular success in Wales. This makes use of diagrams, photocopies of documents, plans, photographs, and even models, which can be successfully spiced with real material from the site like carved stone, as well as audial aids, and there is no doubt that these greatly enhance the visitor's understanding of the remains. There is in an exhibition of this kind a conscious attempt to instruct, which might be regarded as a form of adult education. This opens up the whole subject of the use of ruins for education. By arrangement with the local education authorities many thousands of schoolchildren visit monuments free. There is no doubt a very considerable educational value in displayed ruins, and this use may perhaps be regarded as one of the justifications for the cost of displaying them.

A more exciting form of display is the conscious dramatisation of the ruin by floodlighting or *son et lumière*. The first, which is widely employed, particularly on ruins in an urban setting, gives pleasure to the onlooker and perhaps interest to the town without harming the fabric and may, indeed, attract attention to the monument. *Son et lumière*, devised as it was for châteaux in France, is more difficult to apply to a roofless structure, but a very successful modification used on monastic sites is floodlighting combined with a loudspeaker playing a Gregorian chant.

Bound up with display, although containing elements of preservation or restoration, are the surroundings of the ruin. These are not always within the control of the body which is responsible for the site, but the matter cannot be ignored.

The topography profoundly influences the impression a ruin makes on the mind of the viewer. The drama of the situation is one of the most powerful elements at, for example, Harlech or Beeston or Tintagel Castles, or at Whitby Abbey. In these cases it is the natural formation of the ground that plays the main role, but in others it may be the long-since altered landscape. Too close a proximity to town on a heavily industrialised landscape, as at Conisbrough, Yorkshire, can detract from a castle or abbey. On the other hand, the landscape may have been deliberately altered to enhance the ruins as at Fountains or Rievaulx Abbeys, in contrast to the fine ruin of Kirkstall Abbey in the somewhat unhappy surroundings of the outskirts of Leeds. With industrial monuments, however, traces of the former industry are almost essential for display; the slate-quarry workshops at Llanberis in north Wales would be meaningless without the great slices in the hillside behind caused by the extraction of slate.

The display of a ruin will clearly be greatly enhanced by the restoration of the immediate adjuncts of the original building. This applies particularly to castle ditches, the clearance of which can restore a semblance of fortification, while the reflooding of an originally wet moat can have dramatic results. The sparkle and reflection of water give vitality to a most unpromising ruin. The reflooding of a monastery's fishponds is unusual although could have the same effect. As a rule the treatment of an abbey's gatehouse and precinct wall is all that can be done, and even that is not always possible. Other service buildings, such as barns or watermills and any of the other structures that now survive as earthworks at a ruin but were originally designed for defence, pleasure or practical use, should be preserved and, if possible, revealed more fully. Gardens are a special case. A garden beside a ruin can look incongruous since it implies active occupation, but there may be circumstances, to be described in Chapter 5, when it is justified (see p. 63).

Just as the preservation of a ruin requires the demolition of additions, so its display can be greatly enhanced by the demolition of later obstructions. The most noteworthy examples of this are the walls in many towns (Norwich, Colchester and Hereford among others) which were cleared of later buildings by local authorities in England and by the Government at Conwy, Caernarfon and Denbigh in Wales. In this case also there are problems of decision. The eighteenth-century landscaping at Fountains and Rievaulx is entirely misleading as to the real appearance of these abbeys in medieval times and certainly gives the visitor the wrong impression of their original aspect, but it would be unthinkable to alter it: the landscaping has assumed the importance of a monument in its own right.

The last three chapters have emphasised how preservation and display work have to a great extent been intuitive, apparently almost casual, without rationalisation. It is remarkable that this is the first time an attempt has been made to present an account of the treatment of ruins that has been going on for the last sixty years in Britain. The story is one of characteristic British pragmatism, started in the early years of the century in the flush of the attitude created by William Morris which accorded with the later dominant archaeological ideas; the actual methods of work have been passed on by example and word of mouth, not by written manual.

What, then, should be the objective of display with a treated ruin? Different people will want different things, and all one can hope to do is to provide sufficient information for each to choose what he wants. If the ruin is accessible and intelligible, then the choice must be left to the visitor. All ruins are architectural fragments, and as often as not the architecture is the most expressive feature and needs no further justification. There will be a good deal of necessary architectural history and archaeology, but only for a small proportion of people will this be an end in itself. There is an educational interest, although a ruin is something more than a teaching aid. The most rewarding moments occur when some apparently unintelligible feature is understood or when a feature in the ruin demonstrates a point of general history, not merely the history of that particular site: the division of dorter or infirmary into individual cubicles in the later Middle Ages as the general move away from communal life; the rebuilt corner of the Norman keep at Rochester after mining during the siege; and so on. Then for a brief moment we have a feeling akin to that of Gibbon at Rome; these flashes make the more dreary part of dealing with ruins worth while. The ruin is indeed performing its function as a reminder, a monument in truth.

PART II

4 Retrieval

Restoration—that is, the actual rebuilding of ruins—did not cease at the end of the nineteenth-century; between the wars in south Wales, for instance, very large-scale restoration works were carried out at Pembroke and Caerphilly Castles. At the castle in Cardiff the dazzling reconstructions by Burges were pursued after his death with the completion of the walls of the Roman fort which, together with the buildings of the new Civic Centre erected at the same time, give such a noteworthy heart to an otherwise somewhat drab town. On the hidden internal side the Roman wall face stands to a considerable height, although on the outside only a few courses survived as the restorers have indicated (8). Even if purists have objected to the gallery in the thickness of the wall, the reconstruction remains one of the most noteworthy essays of this kind ever undertaken.

A very far cry from this were the first steps by the Office of Works at Old Sarum and elsewhere just before the First World War to consolidate and lay out ruins unrestored, preserved in the condition in which they were found. Before turning to these activities there is one private piece of restoration work that deserves our attention, carried out more or less simultaneously with the earliest Government essays in this field: I refer to Tattershall Castle in eastern Lincolnshire.

Lord Curzon of Kedleston is chiefly remembered as a politician and Viceroy of India, but he is known to students of ruins for his acquisition and preservation of Bodiam (Sussex) and Tattershall Castles, both now properties of the National Trust. The circumstances of his acquisition of Tattershall Castle, to secure the return of the splendid chimney-pieces after their removal by speculators from the tower, one of the events leading to the legislation of 1913 in which Lord Curzon himself played a leading part, must indeed bring these events into a prominent place in the history of the treatment of ruins. No less interesting was the co-operation in the work of consolidation of an architect, William Weir, and the distinguished young medieval historian, Professor A. Hamilton-Thompson, since it followed a pattern analogous to that in the similar activities of the Office of Works.

It is not necessary to repeat the description recently given elsewhere of Tattershall Castle.[1] An aerial view (9) shows the castle from the west. The broad inner moat enclosed a thirteenth-century castle with round towers, the foundations of which were found during the clearance work. The outer moat and most of the buildings, including the great tower, were the work of Ralph, Lord Cromwell, in the second quarter of the fifteenth century. Brick was the constructional material throughout with stone used for dressings. The great tower with three floors above its vaulted basement and splendid machicolated gallery with four corner turrets rising above is one of the most imposing buildings of the period. Its very puzzling arrangement of doors

35

8 Cardiff Castle, Glamorgan: the rear of the north gate of the Roman fort as reconstructed by the Marquis of Bute with the original work in a lighter colour at the bottom.

9 Tattershall Castle, Lincolnshire: aerial view looking east.

is fortunately explicable by reference to the Buck brothers' print which shows that it had been erected behind an earlier hall. Although arranged vertically in a tower, the rooms seem to have been conceived as ancillary to the hall and, as a result, separate points of access to undercroft, parlour and presence-chamber suite were necessary.

Massive retrieval works were carried out by Lord Curzon. The surface of the interior had been lowered to fill in the moat, and so the earlier foundations were lost. When the moats were scoured out, the inside surface was raised to its earlier level. The outer moat should be concentric, but for convenience of drainage it was returned on either side to the inner moat, not perhaps a very happy solution. The ruins in the area between the inner and outer moats were consolidated but not restored. The appearance of the castle is not unlike one treated by the Office of Works except, of course, for the restoration of the great tower.

As the initial motive for the work was to reinstate the elaborately decorated chimney-pieces, it was clearly essential to protect them from the weather and make them accessible to inspection. There was much in any case in the upper floors that could not be seen from ground level. Roofing and flooring were required and, as a consequence, glazing to protect the new woodwork, which meant replacing mullions and tracery where necessary. Siren calls to the restorer were resisted beyond this except at roof level where crenellations and chimneys were extensively restored. The turrets had had conical roofs, one of which still survived at the time F. H. Reed made his measured drawings in 1872.[2] It is amusing and instructive to compare the reasons advanced for not restoring these conical caps with those so strongly urged by Burges for constructing the improbable 'pepperpots' on the towers at Castell Coch. There could be no clearer demonstration of the change in attitudes between 1872 and 1912.

The prehistoric tombs and earthworks that came into public care in the late nineteenth century did not require retrieval, and the works started early in the present century were rudely interrupted by the First World War. At the end of the war several massive campaigns of retrieval were launched, notably at Goodrich Castle in Herefordshire and Byland and Rievaulx Abbeys in North Yorkshire.

Of the three famous Cistercian abbey ruins, Tintern and Fountains had to some extent been cleared in the eighteenth century (see p. 40), but Rievaulx appears to have been largely a virgin ruin when work began in 1919. A light railway was employed for removing spoil, and the operation must have resembled the exposure of some great tell in the Middle East.[3] The transformation it produced can only dimly be recaptured from old photographs (10, 11). The glory of Rievaulx is the Early English eastern arm of the church and the frater, standing to full height, which were treated when the lower parts were exposed. The point is well illustrated in the photographs where the previously meaningless nave was given dramatic significance by the early 1920s. Most of the cloister, followed by the infirmary, was treated similarly within a few years. Work continued into the 1950s and 1960s on foundations to the south and east of the main conventual buildings. The plan of the ruin has emerged with a remarkable degree of completeness.

Another of the great retrievals of the 1920s was the ruin of the Cistercian abbey of Byland.[4] It is situated not far from Rievaulx, although the comparatively flat country surrounding it, as well as the nature of the remains, make it a much less dramatic

10 Rievaulx Abbey, North Yorkshire: view looking east from the nave before work in 1919.

11 Rievaulx Abbey, North Yorkshire: the same view as no. 10 after treatment.

12 Byland Abbey, North Yorkshire: the nave looking west before treatment.
13 Byland Abbey, North Yorkshire: the nave and cloister area after treatment.

spectacle. The site is dominated by the fragmentary wheel window in the west end, while the church, the main upstanding part of the ruin, is earlier and a good deal more subdued than the eastern arm of Rievaulx. The claustral buildings are much lower, and consequently the ground-plan, which is of great interest, was almost entirely recovered by disinterment of the low walls (12, 13). One of the most remarkable features of Byland is the amount of tiled flooring still surviving. Decorated tile floors are a common feature of monastic ruins and present serious problems of preservation since, as floor coverings within roofed buildings, they were not intended to be exposed to the weather. Although protected by bracken from frost in the winter, their life under the weather and the feet of visitors is not likely to be a very prolonged one.

If one walks through a cathedral in use and imagines it without roof or vault, the problems of preservation in a monastic church ruin become apparent. Plaster is not the only material that cannot survive; sepulchral slabs, effigies and floor tiles are also eroded by the weather. The shining pipes of Purbeck marble turn into repulsive, crystalline lumps. It is impossible, in fact, to maintain an indoors environment satisfactorily out of doors.

Tintern Abbey, Gwent (Monmouthshire), was also the scene of great activity in the 1920s. Set on the bank of the river in the picturesque Wye valley, the surroundings challenge or surpass Rievaulx, but the feeling is very different. This is largely because of the reconstruction of the church later in the thirteenth century: the great traceried windows are in marked contrast to the severe lancets of Byland and Rievaulx (44). The erosion of the mullions and tracery by wind is one of the main preservation problems at the ruin. The plan of the smaller twelfth-century church was revealed during the work, while most of the infirmary and abbot's quarters in the north-east (the cloister is on the north side) have been disinterred.[5] However, the drama of the retrieval at Tintern lies in the engineering work on the south side of the nave of the church, hardly suspected by the visitor.

The nave of the church had originally consisted of a broad central aisle vaulted over and separated from narrow side aisles by six arched openings or bays. After the lead had been stripped from the roof during the Dissolution, the vaults were left exposed and had collapsed. The columns of the north arcade and the wall above had given way leaving the south arcade standing in isolation. The load of superincumbent masonry on the columns right up to the clerestory level was very great, evidently too great for the columns to continue to support it. The ingenious, if laborious, solution to this problem was to build a brick column under each arch which divided in the middle to support the soffit on each side (14). The load of the clerestory was thus taken off the stone columns which could be taken out one by one and replaced by steel stanchions. The stanchions were jacketed in stone using the same moulding as that of the original column (15). The brick columns were then removed and to steady the clerestory further it was anchored back to the south outside wall (where the vault had been), the steel girders being concealed beneath a modern roof. This operation was carried out fifty years ago; its success can be gauged from the fact that few visitors are aware that they are not looking at the original columns.

A number of the large Benedictine abbey churches like Ely, Durham and Peterborough survived the Dissolution and continue to be used for worship today. Some

15 Tintern Abbey, Gwent: pier 3 after jacketing with stone.

14 Tintern Abbey, Gwent: brick support to the south aisle arcade during the removal of pier 3.

have partially survived for parochial use, while others have completely vanished. At Bury St Edmunds in Suffolk the town owes its existence to the abbey whose custody of the bones of St Edmund the Martyr attracted pilgrims just as the remains of St Thomas attracted pilgrims to Canterbury. At the Dissolution there was no need for the church, which was destroyed or, at all events, turned into a ruin. The modern visitor who enters the municipal gardens through the splendid fourteenth-century gatehouse has something of a shock when confronted with the decidedly fragmentary and unprepossessing flint remains of the abbey itself (6). Flint was used in the walls and freestone only for the dressings, but as this was imported it had a considerable value for reuse after the Dissolution in an area lacking its own indigenous stone.

Retrieval which began in the 1950s at the crossing and on the two great transepts of the huge church has continued ever since, extending to the cloister and buildings to the north. Unlike the churches so far described, the eastern arm contained a crypt and there were projecting apsidal chapels from the semicircular eastern end.[6] The remains are so attenuated that it requires an effort to understand what is visible (7). It should be added that the plan had been worked out in considerable detail by A. B. Whittingham before work started, so this daunting enterprise was undertaken for display and not with the prospect of uncovering anything new.[7]

Although there are wide variations in monastic plans between, for example, a Carthusian house and a friary, yet, broadly speaking, if one knows the order one can with fair confidence predict the limits of variation within which the plan will fall. With a castle it is a very different matter: it may be ill-recorded or not recorded at all and in any case it is most unlikely that the records will give any clue as to the original shape. Whereas the monastic plan remained more or less constant throughout the Middle Ages, the plan of castles, always flexible and adaptable to the site, underwent major modification over the same period. For this reason the chances of unexpected discoveries in their retrieval is very much greater than with monasteries. We may begin with a typical example, one of the most unusual discoveries ever made in this field.

Farnham, Surrey, from time immemorial, long before the Norman Conquest, had been a seat of the bishops of Winchester. The first record of a castle there is in 1138, when we are told that one was built by Bishop Henry of Blois.[8] The buildings consist of a dilapidated outer wall with a thirteenth-century gatehouse on its course, and within, crowning the hill, an earlier triangular enclosure with the massive circular keep at its apex. The opposite side of the triangle holds a range containing a hall with a surviving capital of a wooden column in its aisle arcade, and other evidence of twelfth-century work. Dominating the town is the great brick entry tower (redated at the time of the work, see p. 88), now known to have been built by Bishop Wayneflete in 1470–5. All the buildings here are roofed and are not, therefore, our present concern.

The great round keep presented some formidable preservation problems; constructed of soft clunch, its surface was crumbling away. The medieval solution had been to render it over or simply spread the mortar over the surface, although it seemed to have required refacing even then. In the eighteenth century a private garden had been created for the bishop within the interior by forming a staircase in a hole, probably created by 'slighting' in the Civil War. Flower-beds with a raised path ran round the inside of the wall; the mundane object of the work in 1958 was to recover the original surface so that all the superincumbent soil could be removed to relieve the outward thrust against the enclosing wall. Rarely can there have been such unexpected results.

A trench across the interior of the keep seemed to show that at 60 cm or so below the present surface it was all masonry, and only gradually did the full explanation emerge. A tower, 10.5 metres square, was built on the original surface with a well in the middle. It was buried during construction in a mound of hard compacted chalk, and at some 7 metres above the old ground level a flange, 2.1 metres wide, was built out over this mound, evidently to support the battered plinth of a vanished tower above. The tower, 15 metres square, stood in the middle of a conical mound with a truncated surface 27 metres in diameter (16); its two lower floors, dark and windowless below the mound surface with a well in the centre, survive, but its upper storeys (we can guess that there might have been three) that stood in the open have vanished. If Bishop Henry built this in 1138, then it was an adulterine castle of Stephen's reign, and we know that Henry II pulled down the Bishop's castles. This would account for the disappearance of the tower, although to judge by the pottery in the filling of the basement the well was still in use until the end of the Middle Ages. Later in the twelfth century the present great shell of masonry was built, and after the void between its inner face and the mound had been filled, something like the present surface was formed.

Constructed of clunch, the covering over the tower base could not be left open to the weather. Of the interior of the keep only a circular area 27 metres in diameter around the tower is the motte top; the rest is made up of the thirteenth-century filling between motte and later shell.

The discovery is fraught with interest. Something like a thousand of these pudding-shaped earthen mounds, mottes as they are called, are known from the Norman period in England and Wales. Were they all merely skirts concealing basements for towers above? Perhaps the base was normally of wood; the Farnham structure employs a most unsuitable constructional method for stone and seems to imply use of stone for something normally carried out in wood. Certainly anyone who has seen the vast basement at Farnham can never think of mottes in quite the same light again. Unfortunately, few opportunities have arisen since to emulate what was something of an engineering feat in digging down through the mound at Farnham to the original surface.

Roman remains are normally completely buried and have to be disinterred (see p. 22); it is very rare that a medieval ruin in this condition is regarded as suitable for display, but I myself was associated with one notable exception. Bolingbroke Castle, in eastern Lincolnshire, has a particular significance for the Duchy of Lancaster to whom it belongs, since it is the birthplace of Henry Bolingbroke who as King Henry IV created the association between sovereign and duchy that has lasted to the present day.

When they were taken into care in 1949, the remains of Bolingbroke Castle wore a decidedly discouraging aspect: a roughly circular moat was visible enclosing some massive grassy bumps, but no masonry could be discerned. The work of retrieval was

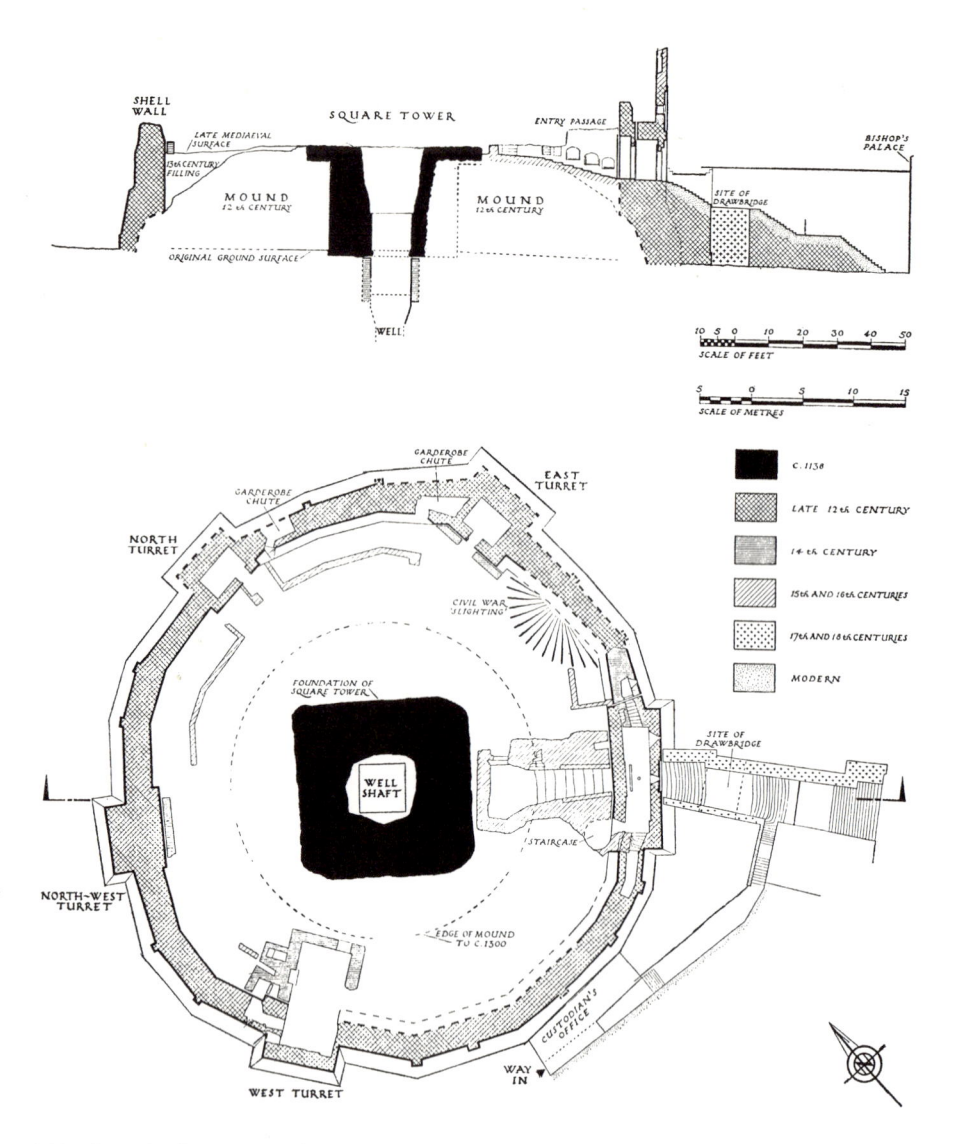

16 Farnham Castle, Surrey: plan and section through the keep.

put in hand in 1965, and we are fortunate that Professor J. K. St Joseph took aerial photographs of the site before, during and in an advanced stage of the work (17, 18), which, apart from flooding the moat, is virtually complete.

The plan of the castle as it emerged from the excavation could hardly be simpler: a massive wall, 3.6–3.9 metres thick, formed an irregular hexagon, the sides varying in length from about 12 to 30 metres, and at each intersection was a large tower, round on the outside and flat at the back. On the north side two of these towers, set about 2.4 metres apart, constituted the gatehouse. The castle is known from written records

44

17 Bolingbroke Castle, Lincolnshire: aerial view in 1953. 18 Aerial view in 1976.

21 Conisbrough Castle, South Yorkshire: aerial view showing the castle after treatment.

to have been demolished in the Civil War, the explanation no doubt for the towers being levelled off at first-floor level. The moat, 30 metres wide, had evidently furnished the material for raising the ground surface within the castle at the time of its construction, and the truncated towers did not rise much above this level. The made-up ground could clearly support only wooden buildings which were no doubt disposed around the courtyard, the lengths of curtain-wall of the towers perhaps being deliberately varied to accommodate the hall and other buildings of different sizes. There are stone foundations of a later hall on the east side.

With such a ruin one must look at the architectural and archaeological evidence first to decide on a likely date for the structure, and then turn to the records to see who owned it at that time. In this case there can be no doubt that the remains are early thirteenth century in date and that the builder was Randulph de Blundevill, Earl of Chester and Lincoln, who was building castles at Beeston, Cheshire and Chartley, Staffordshire, at the same time.[9] This raised the question of an earlier seat which was resolved by the identification of an earthwork a few hundred metres to the north on Dewy Hill, visible on the ground but even more distinct in the air photographs of Professor St Joseph. A very brief excavation in the autumn of 1965 yielded dating material of the twelfth century and so confirmed the assumed date. Unfortunately, the castle is mainly constructed of Spilsby sandstone, which is very friable and tends to revert to its original sand. There can be little doubt that the preservation of the masonry is likely to be a long struggle.

Hardly less remarkable has been the simultaneous retrieval of Montgomery Castle, Powys, just over the border into Wales and within sight of Offa's Dyke. The original eleventh-century castle, an earthen motte and bailey, lay a mile or two to the north and has witnessed some remarkable excavations in the last few years, but the principal monument was a royal foundation of the young King Henry III in 1223, which is well documented.[10] The site chosen—in complete contrast to the contemporary castle at Bolingbroke—a long narrow ridge running north to south—is reminiscent of those favoured by the native Welsh princes, and the great apsidal well tower, the virtual absence of mural towers, as well as the apparent transverse disposition of some of the buildings, reinforce this view. The most significant point in relation to the castle's survival is the record of orders for it to be demolished in 1649 and the record towards the end of the same year that it had been totally demolished.

That this was an exaggeration is indicated by the substantial ruin shown in the view by the Buck brothers. Nevertheless, an aerial view from the north-west taken in 1958 by Professor St Joseph shows only jagged fragments of curtain-wall, well tower and gatehouse (19). The work of retrieval with Mr J. K. Knight in charge of excavations began in 1964; St Joseph's aerial photograph of 1975 taken from the west is impressive testimony to its results (20). The whole ground-plan of the inner ward on the left and middle ward has been exposed, although not yet grassed (and therefore indistinct in the print), and still awaits the oak bridges between the wards.

At Montgomery and Bolingbroke deliberate demolition (and at the latter the weakness of the stone) has reduced the walls to their present sad condition, but nevertheless there is no doubt that the massive walls of keeps and castles can withstand the ravages of time better than the feebler walls of monasteries. Since the early years of the century there must have been scores of castles whose walls have been

19 Montgomery Castle, Powys: aerial view in 1958.

20 Montgomery Castle, Powys: aerial view in 1975.

consolidated and whose low remains of halls and other buildings have been exposed.

Conisbrough in South Yorkshire, its landscape disfigured by coal tips, quarrying and railways, might seem an unlikely place in which a ruin should survive, but in fact the town possesses a most noteworthy ruined castle (21). The site is dominated by a great cylindrical keep clasped by six wedge-shaped buttresses. The whole structure is faced with dressed stone which gives it an elegance more appropriate to France than to England. Attached to the keep at both ends is a much more crudely built rubble curtain-wall with solid projecting towers at each angle rising above it. The keep was most certainly the work of Hamelin Plantagenet in the late twelfth century.[11] On the south side the wall has partly collapsed down the hillside, and as this had happened by the sixteenth century it no doubt prevented the use of the castle during the Civil War and so saved the keep from 'slighting'.

Retrieval of the ruin was begun by consolidation of the upstanding masonry in the 1950s, and it was only in 1967 that the disentanglement of the remains of the domestic buildings within the courtyard was undertaken. Illustration no. 21 shows the castle in 1975 with work completed. The hall with single aisle on the south side on the left was found at the north-west corner with service rooms running eastwards and terminating in the kitchen by the keep. On its south side were a two-storeyed chamber and other private apartments extending to the gatehouse. It proved to be a very satisfying, standard late twelfth-century plan that rendered domestic arrangements within the castle a great deal more intelligible. The vertical movement of the wall on the south side created some bizarre problems of display; the gate being 6 metres lower on one side than on the other leaves the onlooker puzzled, if not incredulous! The discovery of the steps to the entry of the keep led to alterations that will be discussed later (see p. 82).

There could hardly be a greater contrast between the remains left to us from the Middle Ages and those from the Roman period. In both cases the main ruins have resulted from the introduction of alien features, abbeys and castles on the one hand and military works, towns and villas on the other. It is not just the contrast in survival (see p. 9), great as that is, but the contrast with the essentially local nature of medieval remains that impresses: the castle walls as against the villa, the uniformity of the military forts and camps, the relentless course of the roads, the ubiquitous bath-houses so redolent of the Mediterranean, epitomised in the bold portraits of the emperors on their coins (usually from Continental mints) against the crude heads of the Norman kings shown on theirs.

For the preserver of masonry there are several marked differences: the Roman face stones are smaller and squarer although rarely ashlar; there may be bonding courses of tile or other material in the Roman work; the quoin or jamb stones are often of great size with different tooling; and the fine mouldings of the Middle Ages associated with vaults, arcades and windows do not occur. The great contrast, however, is in the mortar which in Roman times was more in the nature of a cement with an admixture of crushed tile. There is no doubt that it is much more difficult to simulate Roman than medieval mortar.

Our first example is the Roman town at Wroxeter, Virconium, in Shropshire on the banks of the river Severn a few miles below Shrewsbury.[12] Although there are a

22 Wroxeter, Shropshire: aerial view of the Roman baths in 1950.

23 Wroxeter, Shropshire: aerial view of the Roman baths site in 1977 with custodian's house removed and basilica under excavation.

few houses within the defences of the Roman town which are clearly discernible on the ground, it is probably the largest of the Romano–British towns not buried under a modern one. There have been extensive excavations there since the early nineteenth century, and so the general plan of the streets and *insulae* into which they divided the town is well known. Aerial views reveal the round stumps of an open colonnade that faced the forum in the bottom of the photographs (22, 23). The only high-standing Roman masonry lies on the axis of the two photographs, near the middle, and is marked by a dark shadow with a hole in it. It is known as the 'old work', a characteristic piece of Roman masonry with tile courses and very hard mortar, which separates the baths on the right from a great aisled building or basilica on the left.

The two photographs show the very small part of the town that has been exposed to public view as it was in 1950 and, after enlargement, as it was in 1977. They speak to a great extent for themselves. The removal of the trees was deliberate to make one conscious of facing the forum. The area has increased in size, and there is a car park and, on the left, a museum which was opened in 1977. On the right the baths have been exposed, the hot baths by the 'old work' and the *piscina*, or cold plunge, with its apsidal ends lower down, while still lower the removal of the custodian's bungalow has allowed the exposure of walls that have been interpreted as belonging to shops. On the left of the 'old work' excavations which are in progress have revealed traces of occupation from just after the Roman period,[13] and retrieval may be described as still going on.

The baths at Wroxeter have presented some tricky problems of display, mainly because the walls have been dug out for the stone to a depth far below the existing surface. The foundations on view in the hot baths are therefore a modern creation, which recalls the technique used in the barrack blocks in the Roman legionary fortress at Caerleon, Gwent, where the original foundation has been buried and a modern foundation created above. It is a moot point whether this can be described as restoration or representation—it is a cross between the two!

The river Tees at Piercebridge forms the boundary between Yorkshire and Co. Durham. The modern road enters the town from the south after crossing the river by a handsome late eighteenth-century bridge, but it has already diverged from the course of the Roman road, Dere Street, before reaching the river. The latter had evidently crossed the river further east on its way north; chance circumstances in the form of gravel-working revealed the remains of the bridge a few years ago, and after their very able excavation by Mr Peter Scott these disinterred remains are now on permanent display.[14] The bridge, the second to be erected, was intended for military use and may well have been erected in the early second century AD when Hadrian's Wall was under construction.

The river at this point is something of a torrent, its volume depending on the season of the year, while its course has evidently moved northward since Roman times. Illustration no. 24 looks southward from a spot near the river soon after the remains were revealed while gravel-working was still in progress and gives a fair idea of their condition when exposed. To understand these we must look at the intact masonry at the extreme southern end (25). The river bed was paved with large slabs following the course of the road, possibly with the initial intention of having merely a ford, but it was turned into a bridge by building masonary piers along it, pointed as cutwaters on

24 Piercebridge, Co. Durham: the Roman bridge exposed by gravel-working.

25 Piercebridge, Co. Durham: the southern bridge abutment after treatment.

the upstream side. The bridge itself was of timber logs or planks, strengthened by diagonal struts, the recesses for which survived in the piers, that spanned the gaps between the piers. The paving of the river bed had been intended to prevent the scouring and undermining of the piers. If so it was clearly unsuccessful, since the jumble of stones becomes more and more chaotic as one moves out into the old river course, a vivid demonstration of the power of the current, especially when the river was in spate.

Hadrian's Wall and its treatment is a subject that deserves a separate volume, for many years of retrieval have been devoted to it. Time has not been kind to the wall: about a third of its eastern end is under the road constructed by General Wade during the 1745 Rebellion, while none of the remainder stands above a quarter or half of its assumed original height, most of it very much lower.[15] Retrieval by unearthing and removal of vegetation is therefore the right description to apply to the form of treatment necessary.

It is in many ways more impressive to see Hadrian's Wall on plan or on a map than it is on the ground, since its purpose as a barrier is at once emphasised by the turrets and milecastles with the forts at greater intervals. The physical remains do not look like a barrier, but the wall's relentless course can still be strikingly demonstrated by the ruin itself—in particular at Heddon-on-the-Wall where retrieval has dramatically emphasised its unchecked progress (26, 27).

To turn to the prehistoric period is to enter a different world altogether. Stone constructions are unusual and dressing of stone unknown (the exception at Stonehenge is so rare as to arouse our wonder). Mortar was quite unknown, and walls survive as dry-stone walling, although some simple adhesive like mud or dung may have been used originally. With modern exposure dry-stone walling can, of course, be strengthened by concealed cement tamping, while concrete beams can be used to support the great capstones of megaliths or hold back their uprights.

The amount of worthwhile information to be derived at a monastery from the mountains of debris accumulated since 1540 is probably fairly limited, but as we retrace our steps into eras where written records grow rarer and finally vanish so, archaeology, as a primary source of evidence, plays a more important part. Evidence of this kind can, of course, only be discovered once, and its recovery, particularly in the early periods where it is the principal source of information about the monument, is as important as the retrieval of the structure itself. Indeed, the main difference between retrieval operations in the 1920s and today is the attention given now to the archaeological aspect of the work. In prehistoric ruins the archaeology has in some measure become the dominant partner and hardly less so in the Roman period, as has been shown at Wroxeter.

Over many areas of highland, that is western Britain, where there was stone to hand it was employed to make low walls, three or four courses high, for circular huts. The superstructure of wood, perhaps covered with turves or thatch, has now, of course, vanished. The hut circles occur from as early as the Bronze Age in Dartmoor but elsewhere are of the Iron Age, continuing in north-west Wales as late as the end of the Roman period. A notable example is on display at Din Lligwy on the Isle of Anglesey. It is the stone which has survived and of which we are most conscious at

26 Hadrian's Wall, Heddon-on-the-Wall, Northumberland, in 1935 (the wall is on the left).

27 Hadrian's Wall, Heddon-on-the-Wall, Northumberland, in 1954 (view taken further east than no. 26).

the site today, but when the huts were in use the vegetable matter such as straw and thatch no doubt made the strongest impression.

A peculiar variety of these structures in which the houses consisted of rooms around a central space occurs in the extreme west of Cornwall, and the next example is the retrieval of a village or cluster of such huts. The excavations at Carn Euny (a few miles east of Land's End) that were carried out by Mrs P. Christie between 1964 and 1972 as part of laying out the remains for display have recently been the subject of a long report to which the reader must be referred.[16] An aerial photograph (Pl. 37 in the Report), shows the hut cluster from the north during the concluding phases of the excavation in 1972 (28). Exposure of the remains and archaeological research went hand in hand with the treatment of the remains. The exceptionally detailed study of the huts has thrown much light on the lives of the people who inhabited them, while radiocarbon dating has revealed when they lived there. The settlement started in the fourth century BC, although the visible remains are later than this, and continued well into the Roman period.

In the centre of the photograph (28) the one small and three large courtyard houses can be seen with simpler round houses to the left and right. Above the nearest courtyard house one can see the deep-cut entry to a long subterranean passage lined with stone and originally covered by large stones, themselves covered by soil. The passage comes out towards the top of the enclosure by the rectangular foundation of a later building. These enigmatic underground structures are known as *fogous* in Cornwall and as *souterrains* in other Celtic areas such as Brittany and Ireland (they do not occur in Wales).

The range of structures at a site like Carn Euny is very small. Structural problems only arise with the *fogou* where the capstones of the roof needed support or methods had to be found to relieve them of the superincumbent load of soil. The low remains of huts require frequent maintenance, and where they are scattered, as at Holyhead, Anglesey, there is a danger of their being overwhelmed by the triumphant bracken![17]

The great communal tombs used for burial over a long period of time, dating from 4000 to 2000 BC, occur in varying forms over much of western and northern Britain. They were some of the earliest monuments to come into care under the first legislation nearly a hundred years ago, but it is fair to say that no works that could be described as retrieval were carried out on them until the 1920s.

There is considerable variation in shape in these tombs, but they all originally consisted of two elements: the chamber or chambers, with or without a passage constructed of large upright stones roofed with horizontal stones, set in a round or long mound or cairn. If the chamber is not differentiated from the passage, we speak of a gallery rather than a passage grave. Where the subsoil was soft, a ditch could be dug on the edge to provide material for a covering mound, but often stones were collected for the same purpose from round about to form a cairn, which was usually demarcated by upright stones or dry-stone walling. The cairn or mound has usually spilled over the edge and hidden it, so one of the principal tasks of retrieval is to redefine the limits of the mound. The uprights of the passage and chamber may need straightening, and it is almost inevitable that the massive capstones will require strengthened support. There may be further complications, such as carvings on the stones (as at Barclodiad y Gawres), or more usually stones have fractured or dis-

28 Carn Euny, Cornwall: aerial view of the Iron Age village.

29 Parc le Breos Cwm, Gower, Glamorgan: the entry to the tomb after treatment.

appeared altogether. When these tombs were rifled in the nineteenth century, a common practice was to use a charge of gunpowder to remove the capstone so as to gain access from the top. In these circumstances it may be desirable to put a concrete top over the chamber and re-create the mound, as has been done at Barclodiad y Gawres in western Anglesey.

The tomb illustrated is at Parc le Breos Cwm in the Gower peninsula west of Swansea (29). It is of a type that occurs on both sides of the Severn Estuary and is known as the Severn Cotswold group. There had been nineteenth-century excavations on the site, but its present appearance is almost entirely due to the work of the Ministry of Public Buildings and Works carried out after archaeological excavations by Professor R. J. C. Atkinson a few years ago. It never looked like this when in use since the top of the cairn has been lost, as well as the capstones of passage and chambers. The excavations have exposed the full plan of passage with opposed chambers set in the end of an egg-shaped cairn demarcated by dry-stone walling. One corner of this has been eroded by a stream. The impounded stones of the cairn have a decidedly artificial look but probably succeed in conveying the semblance of the truncated cairn.

30 Caerphilly Castle, Glamorgan: restored and unrestored windows in the hall.

5 Restoration

If it is claimed that whatever is on view is authentic, that is, belonging to the period of the original construction of the ruin, then surely the need for restoration, in the sense of modern addition, however plausible, should never arise. It is a searching question. Restoration can, of course, be used in the sense of picking up what is already there, like the stones of the trilithon at Stonehenge. Even used in the sense of addition, there may be overriding considerations—structural, preservation or aesthetic—that make it necessary. Let us take the examples in that order.

A very common case is the mullion of a window. This is the moulded upright in a medieval window that may support elaborate tracery at the head. Without the glazing the window opening obviously becomes a funnel for the wind, and erosion will be accentuated. A time will come when it can no longer support the load and has to be replaced with either a substitute (a representation) or a freshly cut mullion, which can be marked to identify it as modern. The same solution may be needed for door jambs, columns or any structural members.

Alternatively, restoration may be necessary to conceal a modern structural support. The columns at Tintern are a case in point (see p. 40). It is far more common to build up core work to conceal concrete beams: the face stones are regarded as sacrosanct, but much more latitude is allowed with the core.

Even in a ruin there is one case where wood can perform an original functional service; it may be necessary to use a doorway to serve its intended purpose. Sometimes a new door or a gate of one or two leaves may have to be made, or alternatively fragments of the ancient wood may survive and the rest of it has to be reconstructed.

As was the case at Tattershall (see p. 35), in order to preserve the chimney-pieces in the tower and make them accessible to view it was necessary to reroof and refloor the structure. Similarly, Caernarfon Castle was entirely ruinous in the nineteenth century before the extensive restoration work which reached a climax prior to the 1911 Investiture ceremony.[1] The fireplaces in the towers survive and the circumstances are similar to those at Tattershall: namely, that the reroofing protects the interior features which would otherwise be exposed to the weather. It is always arguable that where a building survives to full height it is worth reroofing to protect the interior, and if finely carved detail, or still more decorated plaster, survives, the argument is a cogent one.

At Tattershall and Caernarfon restoration was undertaken not for its own sake but to protect exposed features. Restoration resembles the extensions of a telescope: it is difficult to pull out one without pulling out the others. Reroofing usually requires reglazing to reduce wind erosion and draughts. Illustration no. 30 shows the restoration for glazing the windows of the hall at Caerphilly Castle and the tracery after completion. In this case the hall had been reroofed by the third Marquis of Bute, and the intention was to render it usable. There was sufficient evidence for a reliable reconstruction, but the incongruity of the new dressed stone against the old core demonstrates why such restoration is not normally undertaken.

If a structure will achieve a longer life as a used building than as a ruin, why not bring back into use all ruins that stand to full height? There have been notable successes and failures in attempts to do this. Normally three matters have to be weighed. Will the great cost produce a building suitable for the intended purpose? Usually a modern building designed for a specific purpose can be erected at much less cost. Will the mutilations required by modern services such as toilet facilities, lighting, central heating, not to mention new doors and windows, inflict more damage than normal erosion? This is only too often the case. Lastly, if the purpose of a ruin is to remind us of some activity in the past, an entirely discordant modern use can defeat that purpose. One can mention the analogous case of redundant churches where there has been much discussion as to the propriety of using them for residences, petrol stations or bingo halls. This essay is concerned with the use of ruins as ruins, so there is no need to pursue this interesting subject further.

The need for restoration to hold up a structure or protect the stone from the elements is self-evident, but the need for restoration for what might be described as aesthetic or intellectual reasons requires more explanation. A building in use, particularly a public building in ceremonial use, cannot be allowed to fall into decay. If the stone starts shattering or spalling on its face the appearance is such an overriding consideration that probably it will have to be refaced with fresh stone. With a ruin the old stone would simply be brushed and left, since its preservation, not its appearance, is the main consideration. If this austere rule has to be applied to the structure itself, then there is probably a great deal to be said for relaxing it on its surroundings. If the craving of the imagination to restore the ruin cannot be satisfied, at least some of its adjuncts can be restored to stimulate the imagination. The surroundings have a powerful influence on our general impression of the ruin (see pp. 32-3).

The removal of accumulated deposit from a castle ditch is no different in principle from removing accumulated debris from the ruin itself, and the one can have as dramatic an influence on the appearance of the monument as the other. It can be reasonably regarded as part of the preservation work, but if the ditch was a wet one and it is decided to put the water back in it, then it is evidently restoration of a mild kind. It may, in fact, require quite elaborate restoration of sluices and other water controls, and possibly waterproofing of the moat itself.

There are many examples of restitution of moats; one is at Tattershall (see p. 35) which, like Lord Curzon's moat at Bodiam, is a noteworthy case. There are three other particularly interesting examples: Beaumaris Castle in Anglesey, Kirby Muxloe Castle in Leicestershire and Caerphilly Castle in Glamorgan.

Beaumaris Castle at the eastern end of the Menai Strait was the last of the great castles erected by Edward I. Started in 1295, its construction was prompted by the alarm caused by Madoc's rebellion which had led to the seizure and burning of the incomplete castle at Caernarfon.[2] After a few years of intensive work Beaumaris Castle was left unfinished, although in usable condition. It was designed on a grander scale than any of the other castles of Edward I, except perhaps Caernarfon, although it

31 Beaumaris Castle, Anglesey: view along the south side towards the gatehouse before treatment.

32 Beaumaris Castle, Anglesey: same view after excavation and flooding of the moat and construction of the bridge.

is the splendidly geometric ground-plan rather than the low elevations that impresses the visitor.

The great interest of Beaumaris from the point of view of the student of moats is that only about two-thirds of the circuit of the moat have been scoured and reflooded, so it is possible to compare the unaltered part on the east and south-east side with the reflooded moat on the west and north. The impression is even more striking on the ground than it is in an aerial photograph, where the wall on the east side appears more like a boundary than a castle wall.

The fortunate survival of photographs of the south side of the castle, looking eastwards towards the outer gatehouse of the castle, from before, during and after the creation of the moat, allows a vivid picture of the transformation produced by this work (31, 32). The new oak bridge of familiar form spanning the moat emphasises the return of the fortress's original isolation.

The ruin of Kirby Muxloe Castle, Leicestershire, has several claims upon our attention. A fine air photograph (33) shows the sharp regularity of the design of both the internal fortified island and the moat laid out methodically to enclose it. The symmetry of the castle is enhanced by the sparkle and sheen of its attendant moat; an otherwise perhaps not so attractive ruin undergoes a metamorphosis when enclosed within a moat. The castle itself was a rectangular enclosure with square towers at each corner and a great gatehouse in the middle of one side. Brick with stone dressings was used throughout, except in the earlier stone buildings, the footings of which came to light during the retrieval operations by the Office of Works shortly before the First World War.[3] The remains are closely dated to 1480-4 and, apart from the early use of brick, are noteworthy for the fine series of gunports. It must have been one of the last strongly defended private castles erected, or rather partially built, in England and Wales (not Scotland and Ireland) before the Tudor peace.

The construction is exceptionally well documented by building accounts.[4] When the builder, William Lord Hastings, was executed in June 1483, work virtually stopped as soon as the news reached the castle. What is visible in the photographs, the corner tower and gatehouse, was evidently all that was erected, so the castle has always been a ruin from never having been completed. For the moralist the ruin demonstrates the fickleness of fortune or perhaps the fall of pride. There could hardly be a more poignant example to demonstrate not only the architectural interest but also the power of a ruin to act as a reminder of a certain event. The castle incidentally shows how written records of the period can breathe life into otherwise not especially evocative remains.

For the student of ruins Caerphilly Castle has an unequalled interest, both on account of its original history as well as the remarkable restoration works carried out by three different parties in modern times. An artificial lake created for ornamental purposes was a normal feature in the park of an eighteenth-century mansion, but in medieval times the formation of a lake for the defence of a castle by blocking a valley was much more unusual. Leeds Castle, Kent, is one particular case where the lakes have been restored, but the greatest example was the huge mere at Kenilworth Castle, Warwickshire, not yet restored.[5] Gilbert de Clare, who was among the besiegers at the great siege of Kenilworth in 1266, was evidently so impressed by its effectiveness as a defence that he made the erection of a barrage and formation of a lake (the south

33 Kirby Muxloe Castle, Leicestershire: aerial view.

35 Stanwick earthworks, North Yorkshire: the ditch and reconstructed rampart.

34 Caerphilly Castle, Glamorgan: aerial view showing restoration in progress by the Marquis of Bute before the reflooding of the lakes.

lake, the north lake is later) the basis of the design for the new castle at Caerphilly started in the next year. The later history of the castle, including its seizure by Llewelyn ap Gruffud during the construction, and its architectural development have been worked out in great detail by Mr C. N. Johns in the official handbook produced by the Welsh Office.[6]

The third Marquis of Bute, it will be recalled, with his architect William Burges had carried out the restorations at Cardiff Castle and Castell Coch. He was interested in Caerphilly but limited his restoration to putting a roof on the hall (34 and frontispiece). He was able to entertain the Archaeological Institute to dinner there in 1871, as some memorable photographs record. The fourth Marquis undertook the restoration with great zest, demolishing all the houses along the east side and very extensively rebuilding the ruin itself. As can be seen in the photograph, the lake and moats were dry and their reflooding depended on rebuilding the gap in the south causeway where the sluice that controlled the water-level had been. The flooding took place only after his death, when the ruin had passed into the care of the Ministry of Works. The air photograph in the frontispiece gives an idea of the transformation produced in the appearance of the castle by re-forming these large expanses of water to the north and south of the castle.

The visitor to an historic house usually enters up a long drive through a park, and when he arrives there is probably an elaborate garden to see, as well as the house. The great disadvantage of a ruin is that there is often an abrupt, even harsh, transition from road to ruin. The reasons are obvious: monasteries and castles did not have ornamental gardens, and the parks of castles were normally enclosures for breeding and hunting deer. In any case all the appurtenances of a long-since abandoned ruin will have been swallowed up by adjoining properties.

There is an evident incongruity between a garden that implies active use and an abandoned ruin; the restoration of a garden adjoining a ruin is therefore something to be undertaken in special circumstances only and is fairly rare. Three examples can be cited with ground-plans based on diminishing evidence in the order described.

The great Elizabethan courtyard house of Kirby Hall in Northamptonshire, started in 1570 and completed early in the next century, went into a state of long decline and decay in the nineteenth century and was finally stripped of its fittings.[7] When it came into care in the 1930s, it was partially roofed and derelict and partially a roofless ruin. The house had been well known for its gardens in the late seventeenth century; they lay opposite the west front which with its imposing classical pilasters is the most impressive architectural aspect of the house. Some ornamental features were clear, and the kerbstones demarcating the parterres came to light as the undergrowth was cleared. It was therefore feasible to restore the garden, at least to the original design, although the roses and other flowers there now certainly do not correspond to the original planting in the beds. This pleasant garden does something to balance the sad and desolate interior of the house.

At the great castle of Kenilworth the story is different. After the Civil War 'slighting', practically the whole castle, except the northern gatehouse, became an abandoned ruin.[8] Consequently, a good deal of this area was in use as a garden for the occupied gatehouse; the area north of the keep was an orchard. By the early 1970s only a handful of wizened apple trees survived, and so it had to be decided how to replace them. The plan of the Elizabethan garden (probably created by Robert, Earl of Leicester, for the Queen's visit) is shown in Sir William Dugdale's *Antiquities of Warwickshire* (1656), but as the survey had been based on pacing, the measurements were unfortunately too unreliable to be transferred to a modern plan. Excavation produced no trace at all of the parterres, and so the garden that has been formed has been made to correspond roughly to Dugdale's plan, great pains being taken with the planting to use only species likely to have been used in an Elizabethan garden. It is an interesting experiment, although the destruction of the adjoining side of the keep and the curtain on the other side render such a formal layout a little incongruous.

The third example is from Scotland, Edzell Castle in Forfarshire. The site of the garden in the ruins of a courtyard with its niches containing allegorical figures clearly required a central feature. There was no clue as to the original design and what was formed was entirely arbitrary, but no one who has seen it in August when the flowers are in bloom can doubt its success. Authenticity and beauty are by no means the same thing!

An unusual example of restoration for its own sake can be seen in the rampart and ditch of the Iron Age fortification at Stanwick in North Yorkshire. The earthworks represent the defences of the capital of the Celtic tribe of the area, the Brigantes; they can hardly be described as a hillfort since they lie on level ground. The researches of the late Sir Mortimer Wheeler disclosed that there were three phases of construction, each one greatly enlarging the area of the previous enclosure.[9] One of the sections dug through rampart and ditch of the middle phase of *c.* AD 50 was left open, and part of the revetting wall of the rampart was reconstructed over a length of a few metres (35). The onlooker is meant to assume that it was like this all the way round. Although fallen material was used, everything above the few surviving courses at the base is conjecture, that is, both the height and the form of the central piece of parapet. The rock-bottom of the ditch will not have altered, but the sides will have eroded back considerably before they were protected by fallen material.

The reconstruction at Stanwick is a very interesting experiment. It is clearly an aid to understanding the remains, but whether it is worth repeating must be a matter of opinion. The late Sir Mortimer Wheeler was a man of very positive views and knew exactly how he wanted the reconstruction done, but experience elsewhere suggests that the various feasible alternatives can give rise to controversy. In reconstructions of Hadrian's Wall it has been done not on the wall itself but at some distance from it.

The boundary between retrieval and restoration on megaliths is a blurred one. If, for example, one of the uprights has tilted over or the capstone has tipped to one side, is it restoration or retrieval to make the former upright and the latter horizontal? Most people would undoubtedly regard this as retrieval, but if a crane is brought on the site, the stones lifted and put in a separate pile, the stone holes recovered by excavation and then the chamber reconstructed and the mound reconstituted, clearly we are then in the realm of restoration.

In this kind of restoration the archaeologist plays a dominant role, since it is largely upon the evidence that he provides that the reconstruction takes place. The archaeological work will shed a flood of light not only on the date of the structure from the associated pottery or organic material that can yield radiocarbon dates but also on the structural development that took place. Indeed, one is inclined to think that tampering with a megalithic tomb without knowledge of the full sequence of its development can do more harm than good. We tend to think of these tombs as immutable structures, but evidence from the excavations associated with restoration works at Wayland Smithy or Trefignath revealed that the tombs underwent modifications and alterations as drastic as those taken for granted in medieval buildings. The same has been shown to be true of Stonehenge in Professor Atkinson's studies of it since the Second World War.

That the stones at Trefignath, near Holyhead in Anglesey, belonged to a megalithic tomb was generally agreed, and indeed this was why the Office of Works had taken it into care. Since the nineteenth century, however, there has been considerable controversy as to how the stones should be interpreted: did they belong to three separate tombs, or did they form part of one long gallery? From 1977 to 1979 Dr C. Smith undertook a very skilful excavation demonstrating that in effect the chamber was renewed twice in a different form and that there were three chambers, constructed and in use not simultaneously but one after another. The chambers had been rifled, but pottery was found in two of them.[10] The latest chamber is illustrated for another reason in Chapter 6 (40). Instead of a meaningless jumble of stones there will be a structure on display that has a most interesting story to tell.

A suggestive name and a thoughtful landowner, who planted the little copse of beech trees around it, have given to the chambered long barrow of Wayland Smithy on the ridgeway in Berkshire an unusual attraction. After passing into the care of the Office of Works in the last century, retrieval works of a somewhat inconclusive nature were undertaken in 1919–20; much fuller investigations were carried out in 1962–3 under Professors Piggott and Atkinson as part of a fuller restoration.[11]

The excavation identified two entirely distinct phases: a small long mound with flanking ditches, demarcated by sarsens, which covered a collapsed mortuary structure enclosing skeletons; and a long trapezoidal mound, demarcated by upright stones and with its own ditches, covering the earlier mound in its middle, with its own transeptal chambers set in the broad end of the trapeze. A piece of charcoal from clearance by burning before the construction of the main chambered tomb gave a corrected radiocarbon date of 3600 BC + 145.

The discoveries are fraught with interest, more particularly on the question of the relationship of chambered to unchambered long barrows. However, it is restoration which concerns us here rather than interesting discoveries, important as they are for intelligibility in display. Illustration no. 36 shows one of the capstones being replaced over the western chamber after temporary removal during the excavation. Reinstatement of the stones demarcating the edge of the mound (and representation where they were missing) and the formation of a new entry (the original had been blocked in antiquity) by steps down through the side of the passage constituted the main restoration.

Although Stonehenge was cited among the fifty monuments in the United Kingdom (excluding Ireland) in the Schedule at the end of the 1882 Act, it did not pass

36 Wayland Smithy, Berkshire: resetting the capstone over the west transeptal chamber.

37 Stonehenge, Wiltshire: early aerial view showing prostrate stones, which were raised in 1958.

38 Stonehenge, Wiltshire: the lintel of the trilithon being swung into position.

39 Stonehenge, Wiltshire: work completed.

into public care until the end of the First World War. Photographs from 1919 to 1920 show great activity on the site with many shores erected against the stones. The strengthening and underpinning that took place may be regarded as the retrieval stage; since a stone had fallen as late as 1900 there was understandable anxiety about the instability of some of the stones. Almost immediately afterwards Colonel Hawley undertook excavation on behalf of the Society of Antiquaries, which added three new rings of concealed sockets in the chalk to the six visible concentric structures: ditch, bank, lintelled sarsens, bluestone ring, horseshoe of sarsen trilithons and horseshoe of bluestones. The three new rings were the Aubrey holes, just within the bank, and the Y and Z holes closer to the lintelled sarsens (so named because the enigmatic Aubrey holes had also been called X holes). The identification of the place of origin of the bluestones as the Preseli Mountains in Dyfed (Pembrokeshire) at about the same time gave even greater interest to the circles. It was clear from the evidence of reuse on some of the bluestones, as well as the failure of the Avenue to match up with the entry of earth bank and ditch, that there must have been a sequence of alterations; how were these to be unravelled?

The answer came in the early 1950s with the skilful selective excavations of Professors Piggott and Atkinson at the great circle. Three new factors emerged: a pair of concentric rings of sockets used for bluestone uprights and called the Q and R holes, more or less on the line of the later bluestone ring; the identification of excised carvings of flat axes and a dagger; the application of radiocarbon dating to material from the excavation to give exact dates to the changes. Readers must be referred to the valuable books by Professor Atkinson in order to follow the sequence that he has worked out.[12] Period I has the earthwork and Aubrey holes (no posts in them); Period II adds the Avenue and a central setting of bluestones in the Q and R holes; and Period III has the sarsen-lintelled circle and horseshoe as a constant with three subdivisions according to whether there were no bluestones, an earlier arrangement or their existing disposition. The Y and Z holes were for an intended arrangement of bluestones that never took place; it was relatively easy to move the small bluestones about, but alteration of the huge sarsens would have been a much more formidable undertaking.

In some sense the restorations by the Ministry of Works in 1958 and 1959 were the culmination of these intensive researches. It was not a wholesale re-erection of every prostrate stone on the site but the reassembly of one great trilithon of the horseshoe on the west side and one bay of the lintelled circle immediately behind. In both cases the falls had been recorded, the former in 1797 and the latter in 1900. There were even prints and drawings showing the stones as they were before they fell. The two large uprights of the trilithon were estimated to weigh 45 tonnes each, and it required a 60-tonne crane to lift them. A special 4-tonne steel frame with twelve spring-loaded lifting points was employed. It was then a major engineering operation.

In a very early aerial view of Stonehenge the date is revealed by the costume of the visitors in the circle (37). The browsing horses in the foreground help to convey the rusticity of the scene; this was the Stonehenge of which Thomas Hardy had written thirty years before. He had not seen—and it is a significant point—the broken lintel on top of the prostrate trilithon in the foreground since this did not fall until 1900. The camera was pointing directly at the stones raised forty years later: the uprights and lintel of the great trilithon and the stones of the one bay of the outer, continuously lintelled ring of sarsens. Of the five trilithons in the central horseshoe the two on the right (south) are still standing, while of the gigantic one in the middle only one upright with a conspicuous tenon remains. The effect of the restoration was to replace one of the two missing trilithons on the left (north) and one bay of the outer lintelled ring (39). As the whole of the north-western side of the circle is very fragmentray, the improvement in the intelligibility of the plan caused by the re-erection is profound.

Another photograph shows operations in progress in 1958—the lintel being swung into position with engineers on the scaffold ready to receive it (38). The curious objects in the foreground are templates used to make certain that the position of the tenons on the newly erected uprights corresponded to the mortice holes in the lintel. The dressing of the sarsens at Stonehenge, apparently with stone mauls, not only to give the lintels curvature but also to form the grove and dovetail joints on the outer lintels and mortices and tenons on both inner and outer, remains an unending source of wonder. It may be that these are carpentry, rather than masonry, practices, but if so, we can only be the more surprised at how great must be the loss of what was presumably the widespread employment of these techniques in their proper medium, perishable wood. It has already been suggested that in medieval times the structure in the keep at Farnham points to a more widespread use of carpentry for another purpose (see p. 43). These are interesting cases where the surviving stone ruin gives a clue to long-vanished but presumably normal construction in wood.

40 Trefignath, Anglesey: the capstone of the eastern chamber supported on girders while excavation and restoration were in progress in 1977.

41 Carn Euny, Cornwall: the concrete lintel at the entry to the *fogou*.

6 Representation

An alternative choice of word for what is described in this chapter would be 'substitution', but 'representation' has been preferred because it is all-embracing and because it more accurately describes the intention of those concerned with it. Where it is not permissible to restore and where for structural or display reasons one cannot leave a void, a recognisably modern substitute is employed, identifiable at once by the onlooker as modern but of such material as not to be out of harmony with the original ruin.

The thinking behind representation can best be illustrated by an extreme form advocated by the Society for the Protection of Ancient Buildings in their *Notes* of 1903. It was advised that:

> 'The decayed surface of the stone should be cut off, the bed of the stone thoroughly cleaned out, and filled with mortar, and portions of hand-made tiles hammered in so that the straight edge of the tile courses are flush with the wall face ... It will be found that after a little experience the workman will be able with proper supervision to repair decayed mullions and tracery in the same way ...'[1]

The use of tile in this way can be seen on a number of ruins repaired under the aegis of the Society early in this century. When used extensively, it gives the structure a curious appearance as if it were the reused tile on an Anglo-Saxon or Merovingian building. Such a puritanical approach was never adopted by the Office of Works.

Restoration can be used to conceal structural supports, but there may be cases where it is undesirable or impossible to do so. A typical example is a megalith where one of the large uprights is missing. It would be possible to look round for another stone to put in its place, but that would be cheating and misleading—this is the essence of the thinking behind representation—so a modern substitute is employed which could be a girder, a concrete or brick upright, or as in the example illustrated (40) a pillar of mortared stone.

The tomb at Trefignath has already been mentioned (see p. 65). The photograph (40) shows work during the first season with the capstones of the eastern chamber held up on girders while the sidestones were straightened and during extensive excavations, some of which can be seen open in the foreground. The column of built stone had to be put in to replace a missing upright to bear the weight of the capstone when it was replaced. It is an instructive case. The reader will know that mortar was not known in prehistoric times (see p. 52), but this will not be known to all visitors, some of whom will mistake it for part of the original construction. The intention is therefore unexceptionable, to make the representation as unobtrusive as possible, but the whole

71

purpose of the exercise could be defeated if it is so unobtrusive as to be mistaken by the onlooker for the original!

Another example is of a lintel in concrete from the *fogou* (see p. 54) at Carn Euny (41). It was necessary to have a lintel because of the load above, but instead of finding a new stone a shape somewhat resembling a natural stone was made in concrete. Here there is an attempt to imitate the original, which might be described as representation with a hint of restoration.

In conservation of masonry one of the principal objects is to try to conceal the modern beam or support that has been used to strengthen the ancient fabric, and if left exposed, then it is to some extent an admission of defeat by the architect. Obviously there are occasions when it cannot be avoided, but the result is at once to break the illusion and shake the onlooker's confidence. Structural representation is therefore to be avoided and its use is fairly infrequent. Representation is primarily a display, not a structural technique.

The great prehistoric enclosure at Avebury, Wiltshire, is too well known to need illustration here. Starting from the outside, it consisted of a massive bank, then a large ditch, then a circle of large upright sarsens, while within were two smaller stone circles. From one of the four original entrances, and possibly originally from others, an 'Avenue' of parallel lines of stones led away. This is how it was described in the early eighteenth century by the antiquary William Stukeley, but not as it has survived to the present day. The earthworks have survived largely unaltered, but a great many of the sarsens have been removed, buried or broken up by lighting a fire against them and then pouring cold water on the stone.

When the late Mr Alexander Keiller undertook his retrieval works between the wars, it became apparent that Stukeley's plans had been right, since the former position of the missing stones could easily be established from the sockets cut in the underlying chalk in which their bases had been set.[2] If an intelligible design was to be displayed, how then were the positions of the missing stones to be indicated? The solution was to employ low concrete stumps, tapering with pointed tops, as markers. These were used not only within the circle itself but also along the West Kennett Avenue, which had been recorded by Stukeley but was subsequently virtually lost. About a third of the Avenue was explored, and as a large proportion of the stones had disappeared, replacements by concrete markers to represent their former course flank the avenue over considerable distances. The result is a little peculiar but can leave no reasonable doubt as to what was intended.

Although the rest of the Avenue has not been explored, its termination in a circular structure, two concentric stone circles in the time of Stukeley, had been previously investigated by Mr and Mrs Cunnington.[3] Excavation revealed that there had been not only concentric circles of stones but also concentric circles of long-since vanished wooden posts, the sockets of which are the 'post-holes' of archaeologists. Here, then, the task was to represent the subterranean evidence for uprights of two kinds, and this has been done by rectangular concrete markers for the positions of stones and circular concrete markers to represent wooden posts. The low projection of the markers and the lack of elevation for the onlooker makes it difficult to see the design, but it is not an unsuccessful solution.

The ultimate in representation is Woodhenge, the prehistoric site further south in Wiltshire, a series of concentric rings of post-holes within a bank and ditch discovered from the air and excavated before the Second World War.[4] As it was thought that the posts had been lintelled to each other like the stones at Stonehenge, it was christened 'Woodhenge'. Here, low concrete bollards, varying in diameter to represent the variations in girth of the original posts, have been employed (42). The result is peculiar, but it serves its purpose well enough. As the height of the original posts is quite uncertain and there is considerable controversy as to whether the structure was roofed or not,[5] an impassive representation of this kind leaves these questions open.

We have so far been dealing almost exclusively with prehistoric remains, for it is with these that the most extreme forms of representation are employed. It would be quite wrong, however, to think that representation is not used in later ruins. It is employed in fact to convey a message: there ought to be something there but it has vanished; or there was something earlier than what is visible and it is indicated in this way. Representation, modern material in an ancient structure, is quite distinct from 'allusion' in a modern building, like tiles over the roof of a museum at a Roman site, or that brilliant and original proposal some years ago for building a restaurant over the river at Fountains Abbey, recalling the infirmary over the river in the monastery. This, however, represents a move into the field of original design and away from the more bread-and-butter fare of the preserver at a ruin.

Let us consider the only too common occurrence at a ruin of a jagged hole in a wall. It may be that there was an original window or door which has been enlarged for other purposes, a very frequent mutilation. The great hole in the old work at Wroxeter may have been created by enlarging the original doorways to the baths to allow access for carts. There is not much to be done about it; but suppose the masonry above needs support, or the wall forms the boundary of the property? Clearly the hole must be filled, and this can be done by a recessed blocking, if necessary of brick rendered over, which is patently modern and conveys the message that it has been done without prejudice as to whether there had or had not been an original opening in this position.

42 Woodhenge, Wiltshire: the concentric rings of post-holes represented by concrete bollards on the surface.

A common case is where there is a need to represent the shape or position of earlier buildings that have preceded the visible ones on the site and are important for their history. A good example is the parish church at Jarrow, Co. Durham, which is still in use. Its chancel is an original Anglo-Saxon structure, its nave a modern rebuild replacing what is known to have been of the seventh century, and the two elements are linked by a Saxon tower. South of the church are the remains of the claustral buildings of the Norman monastic foundation. The church is in a very exposed position on the estuary, and it may therefore be assumed that the famous monastery associated with the Venerable Bede was destroyed by Viking marauders at an early date. During the lapse of time between this destruction and the re-foundation of the monastery the original conventual buildings had vanished. Since the monastic cloister plan, as we know it from the high Middle Ages, is a creation of Carolingian times, it was fairly certain that the Anglo-Saxon buildings were not arranged around a cloister; beyond this, however, nothing was definite. In the mid-1960s Professor Rosemary Cramp carried out excavations on the south side of Jarrow church that threw a good deal of light on the matter.[6] South of the church and parallel to it she found well-built foundations of two aligned rectangular buildings. They were, of course, at a lower depth than the later monastic walls, some of which existed only as foundations.

The problem, then, at Jarrow was to represent the Anglo-Saxon foundations (clearly the most important period on the site) without hopeless confusion with later remains. The original masonry could not be exposed without lowering the whole surface of the ground, and in any case the masonry would be much better preserved under the ground. It would have been possible, as at Caerleon and Wroxeter (see p. 50), to have re-created the foundations at a higher level, but this would have caused confusion with later remains. The first solution was to use concrete kerbs retaining gravels of different colours, but these tend to fade. In the present solution paving slabs for the earlier period contrast with pointed or unpointed setts for the later periods (43). Changes of mind in a field where tastes vary are likely to be common.

At Jarrow there was a hiatus between the earlier and later structures, but it was more

43 Jarrow, Co. Durham: the position of buildings of different date marked out in the later cloister.

usual for there to be continuity. One will sometimes see marked out on the floor in the eastern arm of a cathedral in use the original end with its apse before an eastward extension. One of the most remarkable examples of this in a ruin is in the great earthwork of Old Sarum, the predecessor of Salisbury which lies a mile or two to the north of it. Before its transfer to the modern site early in the thirteenth century, the seat of the bishop and the cathedral lay within the earthworks on the north-west side; the foundations were excavated in the early years of the century and are now on display. They are decidedly fragmentary, so mortared gravel of two different shades has had to be used to represent the original eleventh-century cathedral and its huge extension under Bishop Roger in the early twelfth century.[7] Had this been a monastic church, the exiguous remains might not have been worth laying out, but in this case the position of the cathedral is clearly essential to the understanding of the Norman town on the hill.

Monastic churches underwent similar alterations, indeed often greater when unforeseen increases in the religious or bequests required wholesale reconstruction. At Rievaulx the eastern arm was rebuilt, while at Tintern the whole church was rebuilt on a vastly greater scale. The earlier form of the church that came to light during retrieval is now marked out by concrete kerbing. Cistercian houses suffered from other problems of overcrowding owing to the large number of lay brothers. This is why the frater on the south side of the cloister was swung through 90° to allow more room, but it is only in rare cases, as at Tintern, that evidence survives for the east/west frater before the alteration was made.

There are a number of different ways of representing missing features on the ground. Concrete is the representer's material *par excellence*: on a close-cut lawn the most convenient way of representing missing features is to lay the concrete flush with the ground, so that the mower does not fowl a projection. The snag is that the grass tends to close over it and the marks disappear altogether. Projecting kerbs are more conspicuous, particularly if the intervening space is filled with gravel. Gravel raises maintenance problems because it is inevitably kicked on to the grass and can damage mower blades. There is a harshness and modern appearance about concrete which lends itself to representation, whereas natural stone (slate perhaps less so) tends to have a rockery look about it. Paving or solid concrete tends to look like a garden path.

The degree of emphasis can be varied. For example, the sites of missing piers in an arcade visually demand more emphatic treatment than an earlier east end which is probably understood only by the learned onlooker and is a source of confusion for the ordinary visitor. The missing piers require gravel infill, the earlier east end reticent lines in the grass. Sometimes in a ruin it is not clear to the onlooker which part was originally roofed and which was open to the sky. Differentiation can be made by using gravel for the former and grass for the latter. It is not an ideal arrangement since it can be misunderstood, and so is best reserved for situations where some kind of differentiation is essential.

The subject of representation is perhaps more suitable for a manual or textbook. It is indeed to some extent a question of trial and error with no hard and fast rules. The more fanciful the solution attempted, such as trees to represent missing piers in an arcade, the more unhappy the final result is likely to be.

44 Tintern Abbey, Gwent: aerial view across the river Wye showing the new entry.

7 Access

By the term access we mean both the approach to the ruin, as well as access to parts of it after entering. The two are, of course, different matters and will have to be taken separately.

The owner of the country house controlled a considerable area of ground around it and so could have the principal approach facing the main façade or alternatively entering at the back. In the case of a ruin it is purely fortuitous whether the modern entry corresponds to the original. It is more common with castles than with abbeys: one need only mention a few surviving examples of abbeys like Thornton, Bury St Edmunds or Battle to realise how uncommon it is. In a great many cases the gate-houses and precinct walls have completely vanished. Clearly the illusion for the visitor is greatly heightened if instead of entering through a hole in a wall he enters through the original gatehouse. In practice this may require years of waiting to obtain adjoining property and is often not attainable at all. The relentless pressure of the motor car may assist, or may make it an unattainable goal. In the two cases discussed here the congestion of cars was the prime mover, but the results were very different.

At Tintern the course of the early nineteenth-century road from Chepstow to Monmouth cuts across the former great court of the abbey, separating the abbey itself from its gatehouse, now indicated by the remains of the gate-chapel. It would not, therefore, be possible to restore the original entry without moving the road. The visitor who parked his car at the west front and then entered the conventual buildings through the outer parlour was following the proper medieval entry. The difficulty was that as the number of visitors rose so the space required for parking at the west end of the church grew larger. We tend to think of abbey ruins in an eighteenth-century landscape, as at Rievaulx and Fountains, and so the proximity of the cars to the abbey is offensive. A partial solution to this problem has recently been worked out by transferring the entry to a hidden point by the river Wye on the side of the abbey, where it has been possible to erect a large new building with ample space for sales, toilet facilities, interpretative exhibition and so on (44). This is a utilitarian solution without any pretension to restoring an original entry, since the visitor will now enter at the north side of the cloister. It is an example where practical considerations have had to hold sway over historical ones.

In no two ruins are the problems of approach the same, and although the initial reasons for altering the entry may be the most mundane, there is sometimes the possibility of turning it to account historically. At Conwy Castle in north Wales the absence of toilet facilities and the impossibility of installing them in the ruin gave rise to the most ingenious proposal of a bridge entry on the original lines with this necessary facility provided at the bridgehead.

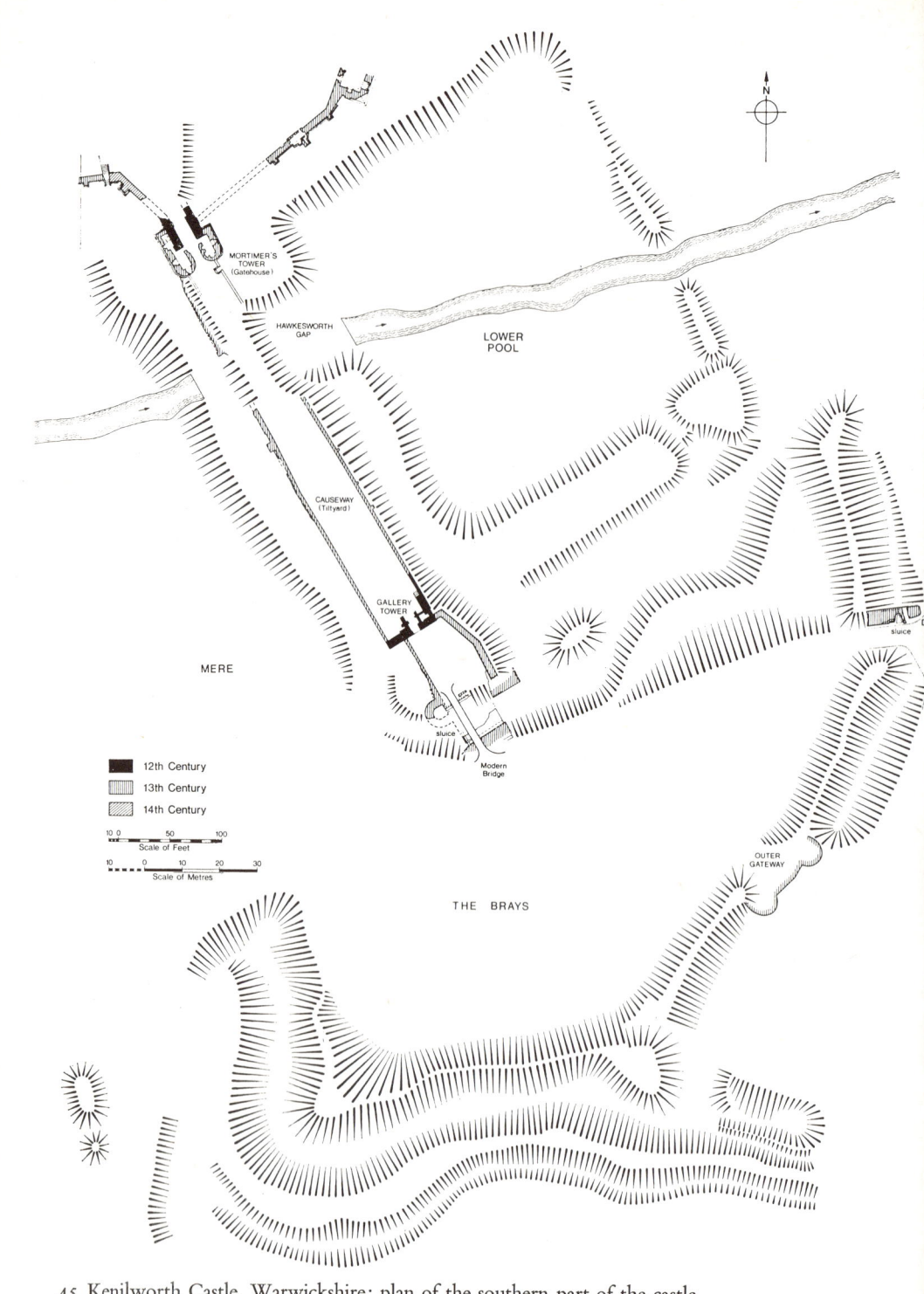

45 Kenilworth Castle, Warwickshire: plan of the southern part of the castle.

46 Kenilworth Castle, Warwickshire: concrete bridge linking the Brays to the dam.

47 Harlech Castle, Gwynedd: arrangements at the entry in 1979.

Kenilworth Castle in Warwickshire straddles a valley, the two parts linked by a massive causeway that acted as a dam to pond the great artificial lake on its west side known as the mere. The lake had existed from the time of the foundation of the castle in the twelfth century, but it was greatly enlarged and deepened in the early thirteenth century when its eastern edge determined the line of the western curtain-wall of the castle.[1] The evidence for this came to light during works described below. The main castle is on the north side of the valley, while an earthwork enclosure known as the Brays is at the southern end of the dam. Medieval access was across the moat at the south-east corner of the Brays, over a bridge on to the dam, through gatehouses at its southern and northern ends and so to the inner castle to the north. There was only a small postern gate at the northern end of the castle, itself discovered at this time since it was buried under the ground.

The whole situation was altered when the Earl of Leicester decided to erect a gatehouse at the north end, to turn the back of the castle into the front, as Dugdale put it. The southern entry remained in use; this was the entry Queen Elizabeth used on her famous visit in 1575. The real break came with the Civil War, since the castle then became ruinous, except Leicester's gatehouse which was converted into a house. The southern entry was now superfluous, while the gap made in the dam to let out the water rendered it unusable.

The problem confronting those with charge of the castle was that the volume of cars that needed to be parked could not be accommodated in the park at the north end. It was a very familiar situation. As a result, it was decided to use the Brays as a car park, which meant, in effect, that the medieval entry by the south end was to be restored. Four or five major works were involved, of which three concern us here (45).

First, the gap in the dam made in the Civil War had to be blocked so that pedestrians could walk along it. Simply to have filled it in would have ponded the stream and re-created the medieval mere! The solution was to put in three great pipes through which the stream could pass, while the dam itself could be reconstituted above. An opportunity was taken to cut back on one side to expose the make-up of the dam, which lent weight to the view that it was not a single work but had been raised very substantially to increase the size of the mere.

At the southern end of the dam exploration revealed two phases of gatehouse, a large southward extension having been built when the mere was raised in order to protect the water controls. The key item in these had been a set of wooden lock gates which had, of course, disappeared. The overflow channel on the south side was of great interest, since it revealed the maximum level of the mere, an important matter if the intention was to reflood it (46). That there had been a bridge here was evident, but it was not possible to decide on its original form. In the circumstances the gap which could not have been spanned by an unsupported wooden bridge was crossed by a single-span concrete bridge (see pp. 30–1).

It was decided not to use the original entry to the Brays but instead to make use of the modern break in the earthwork made for a minor road to a farm. Works were necessary to make this suitable for large vehicles, and it was found that the northern side extending across the outer ditch consisted of a massive masonry structure with an aperture in it, evidently serving as a sluice. The great difference in water-levels

48 Conisborough Castle, South Yorkshire: the modern steps to the keep.

49 Caerphilly Castle, Glamorgan: bridge linking the west side of the castle to the island.

between the eastern and western sides of the castle must have required controls of this kind at its north and south ends.

The new car park at Kenilworth is an instructive example of how a most prosaic requirement can lead not only to an impressive restoration of an original approach to a major ruin but also to a rich harvest of historical information about that ruin, together with the tangible remains related to that information.

While a castle was in use it was obviously necessary to put as many obstacles as possible in the way of an enemy trying to gain access: moats, drawbridges, portcullises and so on. When the castle no longer had a defensive function, such obstacles were a nuisance to be eliminated. Consequently the only evidence today for the portcullis is the grooves in the wall on either side in which it moved up and down, while the position of the drawbridge is marked by a recess or a hole for the chain that raised it. The drawbridge pit, or the pit for the counterpoise weights for the bridge, has usually been filled, but has subsequently been cleared out when the ruin was taken into care and is visible to the visitor peering down from a modern wooden bridge. This is usually the case, but two very interesting examples deserve our attention.

Harlech Castle on its rock overlooking Cardigan Bay is a sight, once seen, never forgotten. Of the three castles begun by Edward I in the spring of 1283, all designed presumably by James of St George from Savoy, it was completed like Conwy in about six years but differed from both Conwy and Caernarfon Castles in three respects.[2] It is more or less square; it is 'concentric' with a low outer wall; it had no attached walled town. Our attention, however, should be turned to the great gatehouse on the east side and the smaller opening through the outer wall in front of it.

Until 1960 the castle was entered by a solid masonry causeway across the great rock-cut ditch on the east side, an extremely easy method of access, but it was known that this modern causeway concealed the stumps of medieval structures that had dominated the approach. These had consisted of two towers of differing height in line with the gate, with a solid stone bridge between them and drawbridges in front and behind. Once the stumps had been freed from the stonework of the modern causeway, it would have been possible to put a wooden gangway above them. Apart from putting this directly in front of the great gatehouse there was the further problem of a sales point. The solution adopted was to hide the new sales building in the ditch further north, so that the visitor then turned through an obtuse angle to go up a diagonal gangway to the gatehouse (47). The two aims were achieved at the cost of a rather more devious entry to the castle.

The work of retrieval at Conisbrough Castle, South Yorkshire, has already been mentioned (see p. 48). The great cylindrical keep like other Norman keeps has its door on the first floor (21). It was evident that the stone steps that rose straight to the door were relatively modern, and during the excavation the base of the original entry steps came to light. They were at right angles to the modern ones, parallel to the face of the keep, terminating evidently in a platform some 3 metres away from the door of the keep. The intervening space would have been spanned by a movable gangway or bridge. Having removed the modern steps, the next question was what to put there instead.

50 White Castle, Gwent: bridge to the inner ward as first installed.

51 White Castle, Gwent: the new bridge completed.

The first solution proposed was wooden steps continuing the surviving stone ones upwards and ending in a landing in front of the door. One difficulty, a perennial one, was that medieval people were prepared to tolerate much steeper steps than are acceptable today. The main snag was the large number of timber uprights that would have been required to support such a structure, forming an ugly forest of timbers. The solution adopted can be seen in the photograph; it has abandoned timber altogether and by the use of concrete has made a much lighter structure leaving the original arrangements clearly visible (48).

In discussing the retrieval at Beaumaris a photograph showed the reflooded moat at the gatehouse with its wooden entry bridge (32). Sometimes these oak bridges leave a strong impression on the ruin, like the two bridges at either end of the castle at Helmsley, Yorkshire. Illustration no. 49 shows an elaborate example at the west end of the castle at Caerphilly linking it to the island enclosure.

Problems arise if the span is wide and the depth great, since a wooden bridge needs frequent support and tall uprights need bracing. If the stone piers of the original bridge are missing, this can create difficulties. It can be circumvented by recourse to that invaluable ally, ferro-concrete, either to replace the bridge altogether or as a concealed support for timber. The most dramatic use of concrete is the sectional bridge at Beeston Castle, Cheshire, that rises in a parabolic curve to the gate of the inner ward, while the more staid one at Kenilworth has been described (46). These examples do not alter the incompatibility of concrete and natural stone. On the other hand, support for the bridge's wooden decking by a horizontal concrete beam has come into general use. With an oak handrail the bridge gives the impression of being held up by magic! Photographs of the bridge to the inner ward of White Castle, Gwent, show it in its pre-war form with tall timber supports, then its replacement completed (50, 51).

The styles of oak handrail on bridges are normally repeated where guardrails or external staircases are needed. The external first-floor door is a perennial problem on medieval ruins, not only in keeps but also in normal first-floor halls and other secular buildings.

Ruins are distinguished from used buildings chiefly by the absence of wood, but what has to be appreciated is the altogether more important part played by wood in medieval than in modern times. It was a question not only of roofs, floors and doors but also of screens, furniture, crockery, window shutters, pentices or lean-to passages, gates, bridges, carts, minor or even major buildings, fuel and so on. What would have struck a modern visitor to a now-ruined castle in its original state would almost certainly have been the pervasive presence and smell of wood. Only the skeleton, the masonry, has survived, and the flesh and blood of the structure which was in wood has vanished. If, then, the oak bridges help even slightly to redress the balance, they are serving a useful purpose besides their more obvious function.

8 Interpretation

'Interpretation' can be used in two senses: primary interpretation, in which someone has to confront the ruin and give an intelligible account of it, usually embodied in the 'official guide' or 'standard handbook';[1] secondary interpretation, that is, the popular transmission of this account, or the more interesting parts of it, to other people. The latter is in part an educational function and requires different skills from the former with which we are concerned in this chapter.

When confronted with a ruin how does one set about understanding it? There are two main ways of doing this: by looking at the remains themselves and by going to the library to find out what other people have written about them. If it is a large or famous ruin, there will almost certainly be a great deal written about it. Let us take the tangible evidence first.

The earliest ruins belong to a period when the people who erected them could neither read nor write, the period before written records or prehistory as it is called. This is fairly easily understood by those familiar with modern primitive peoples in the same condition, but it is by no means readily understood by the layman, who tends to ask about the history of this neolithic tomb or that Bronze Age barrow without fully realising that people lived long before they could read and write.

We are not of course helpless in the face of such a ruin. This type of tomb is found two miles away, and there are a score of others within twenty miles; they have all yielded this particular type of pottery; skeletons have been found in some; science has provided radiocarbon dates of 4000 and 3000 BC for two of them. There is no need to elaborate on the methods of prehistoric archaeology; it suffices to say that a great deal can be said about a prehistoric ruin, albeit of a somewhat impersonal nature.

The evidence will be almost as impersonal from a Roman villa, since although there is a broad historical background for the Empire the names and lives of the users or owners of the site will be quite unknown to us. There may be inscriptions and there will certainly be coins which, together with the profusion of pottery, will allow a very precise sequence to be built up. It is a rigorous exercise that leaves the emotions little stirred.

If a silent film of 1924, a film of 1944 and another of 1964 are compared, the differences between the costume, furniture, motor cars and behaviour and those of today are what at first strike us, but no less significant are the differences between themselves. With a little practice one can date the films from the hair-style, costume, motor cars or behaviour. This is what the archaeologist is trying to do over much longer periods of time. Both rest on the assumption, a fairly self-evident one, that there is continual change, slower no doubt five or six centuries ago but still unceasing, and that there will be regional variation, far greater in the past than today. The film made in the 1920s in Germany or Japan will differ markedly from that made in Hollywood. The surviving physical remains will, of course, reflect not only moments in this change but also spots in its regional variation; this is what archaeology is all about. Ruins are a particular kind of frozen evidence from one or perhaps several of the points in this unending change. From the decoration and techniques employed in the ruin it should be possible to infer the date, from the plan its purpose and from its purpose something about the society that erected it.

'Medieval archaeology' has sometimes been regarded as a post-war creation, and in the sense of digging things up this is probably true, but in the sense of understanding medieval buildings nothing could be further from the truth. One of the great intellectual chasms between the eighteenth and nineteenth centuries is that in the latter the viewer had a fairly clear idea of what he was looking at when examining a ruin; in the former he had scarcely any. So long as the twelfth-century arch was attributed to King Alfred, the picture in the mind was a hopelessly misleading one. The scheme of Thomas Rickman (1776–1841) and its confident linking in some cases to documentary sources need no description here; it created a conceptual framework for looking at any medieval structure even where no documentary sources survived. The overweening confidence of the restorers in the last century was in no small measure due to the dramatic advances in knowledge of medieval buildings in the previous two or three decades.[2]

This brings us to a fundamental point that is not always grasped: some assessment of the architecture of a ruin must take precedence over any attempt to link the remains with the documents. If the monastic annals tell us that the first church was erected in 1140, it is clearly most unwise to attribute the existing church, patently of 1300, to the original foundation. The first church must have been pulled down and replaced. It is just as unwise to attribute the fan-vaulted aisle to a thirteenth-century abbot. This is an elementary point which is not easily grasped by the ordinary person; furthermore, it affects the whole of one's historical picture of the ruin. There is no point in imagining William the Conqueror in a stone castle, when in his time castles were built of earth and timber.

There is perhaps a clue here to the marked reluctance of some academic historians to take cognisance of ruins; it is as if the freer flow of the imagination allowed by written sources is obstructed or constrained by the tangible remains of the period. This has found its most remarkable expression in the official guides where the history is written by one author and the description by another.

Study of the relationship between written sources and visible remains is like the reciprocating action of a piston. The documents may point to some period of great prosperity or alternatively to a period of great poverty, and so one will seek evidence for active building in the former or decline and demolition in the latter.[3] Medieval structures can be only approximately dated, so the degree of certainty with which associations are made can, to put it mildly, be optimistic. The best basis for understanding a ruin is therefore a wide knowledge of other structures of the same period, whether ruined or not, since the mind is consciously or unconsciously making comparisons, and the larger the stock upon which it is possible to draw, the more reliable the result is likely to be. For reasons that will be fairly obvious from Part I it is during retrieval that the attention is most firmly held by the new aspects or discoveries revealed in the work. Ideally, someone present during the retrieval should therefore do the primary interpretation, although in practice this is often not possible.

It is not necessary to itemise or catalogue the written sources available for ruins, since that would provide material for a separate book; yet it is a subject that calls for some comment. First, there are secondary sources—descriptions by people who saw the ruin only as it was after it had passed out of use. These will have been studied before retrieval to assess the importance of the monument. There may be descriptions or historical accounts by Leland, Camden or later antiquaries, articles in journals of learned societies or, if one is very lucky, in those ambitious projects born in the early years of this century, the *Victoria County Histories* and *Inventories of the Royal Commission on Historical Monuments*, and still not concluded. It is important to remember that a ruin is a constantly deteriorating structure and a print or description made two hundred years ago may show much more than survives today. Reference has already been made to the Bucks' views (see p. 15). To this extent a secondary source becomes a primary one.

The use of primary or contemporary sources from Domesday to Tudor times requires some historical skill in understanding what can be legitimately inferred from the document and what cannot. The fact that no castle was mentioned in the 'Domesday Book' in 1086 does not mean that there was no motte-and-bailey there at that time, since the scribe was concerned with the value of the manor rather than with the form of the residence. The account by Gervase of the introduction of the Gothic style into Christ Church Cathedral, Canterbury, is to be trusted because he was an eyewitness, but his account of events at Durham and in Ireland are to be treated with circumspection as he had his information at second or third hand.

The pitfalls are greater perhaps with monastic chroniclers than with the immense volume of medieval royal records that has come down to us. A very substantial part of these records has been calendared, that is, translated into English and indexed. In so far as they refer to royal building operations they have been employed to form the two first, medieval volumes of the *History of the King's Works*, which constitute such an invaluable backbone for the study of ruins of secular buildings during the Middle Ages. Because of the continuity of government and administration since the Middle Ages the records give us a wealth of information on official buildings, mainly castles, from the middle of the twelfth century that is without parallel in the rest of Europe. How different from the monasteries, whose libraries were pillaged and whose records were destroyed in a few short years at the Dissolution!

If it is intended to go all the way in the interpretation of the ruin, it will be necessary to pass beyond printed sources to original manuscripts. Although an enormous amount of manuscript material has been printed, it may well be that certain aspects of the ruin's history, quite possibly the accounts recording its construction, exist only in manuscript. Here the technical aspects of being able to read and understand the manuscript become of paramount importance. An original record, rather than its modern representation in print, gives correspondingly greater pleasure and excitement.

The nature of the written evidence, or the lack of it, will have a considerable influence on our attitude towards the ruin. A monastery, for example, was specifically founded with the object of allowing the religious within it to withdraw from the world outside; it is sometimes said that an abbey had no history between its foundation and its dissolution. This, of course, is an exaggeration, for the world would in fact irrupt into it: there were financial ups and downs, building operations, the election of abbots (like Abbot Samson), their deaths. There is, nevertheless, some truth in this, which, combined with the loss of building records, gives a monastic ruin a kind of detachment. As medieval architecture found its highest expression in ecclesiastical buildings, it will be understood why this type of ruin is particularly attractive to those with an architectural bent and repels those whose interests are primarily documentary.

It is not only royal buildings for which building accounts survive. They may be attached to manorial accounts (see below), or there may be records of building expenditure within the manorial account itself. The great series of rolls of the Bishops of Winchester, each roll an annual record of the fifty odd manors of the Bishop, starting from the reign of John, have proved an invaluable quarry of prices and wages for economic historians. In addition, they contain records of expenditure on building and it was from these books (not rolls by this date) that I was able to redate the great brick tower at Farnham Castle to 1470–5.[4] The building account (provided the building is correctly identified) is a record of the previous year's expenditure on the structure, the fragments of which constitute the ruin being interpreted. Unlike an instruction about which there can be a change of mind or which can prove impossible to carry out, an account is retrospective and so in ruin studies must be regarded as the ultimate authority.

How our understanding of a building can be deepened by the survival of accounts of expenditure on its construction has already been mentioned with regard to Kirby Muxloe, Leicestershire (see p. 60). It can be contrasted with a case like the keep at Conisbrough which is totally undocumented. It is extremely instructive to compare Caernarfon, the great royal castle of north Wales, as it is described in the official guide, with Caerphilly, the great castle of Gilbert de Clare in south Wales, as described officially. The first relies on contemporary royal records and teems with figures of expenditure, while the second has very little written evidence upon which to draw but links such as there is with minute architectural analysis.

From an interpretative point of view the great advantage of a secular ruin, like a castle or manor house, over a monastic ruin is that an individual owner once existed. The descent or ownership can be traced from legal records so that the structure can be linked with a name about whom a good deal may be known from other sources. The descent is to some extent a history of the site, although a long recital of owners' births, deaths and marriages does not often throw much light on the ruin itself. Indeed, too much concentration on family history can arouse the suspicion that material on the structure itself is deficient!

Ideally, this chapter should conclude with a long series of examples to illustrate the points that have been made. In fact, over a lifetime an individual is unlikely to acquire this degree of knowledge on more than a handful of major ruins, and in an essay of this kind it would be inappropriate to expand the examples beyond reasonable limits. In the three cases chosen retrieval has been completed at Pickering Castle and Higham Ferrers but is still in progress at South Wingfield Manor.

Pickering is a small town in Yorkshire, a few miles north of Malton at the foot of the North Yorkshire Moors, on the north side of the Vale of Pickering. The castle, which belongs to the Duchy of Lancaster, was placed in the care of the Office of Works before the Second World War; the well-groomed appearance of the grass shows that work had been completed when the air photograph (52) reproduced on p. 89 was taken in the 1950s. In the foreground is the railway, the castle in the middle distance with the Nissen huts of an old army camp beyond. The roofed building in the near part of the castle is a chapel, so we are looking eastward along its ridge. The most prominent feature in the photograph is the great conical mound of plum-pudding shape in the middle of the picture with fragments of masonry (a 'shell keep') on top, linked to walls that divide an inner enclosure ('ward') on the left from an outer 'ward' on the right. There is, indeed, a classic simplicity about the design.[5]

The North Riding volumes of the *Victoria County History* covered the castle's history in some detail, while the defunct North Riding Records Society had devoted its only four volumes to the Duchy records of the castle. From the point of view of assistance in coverage of the records one could hardly ask for more. In fact, to judge by the later account in the *History of the King's Works* which goes over the same ground the only significant omission was the year's expenditure on the outer curtain-wall in 1324–5.[6] The castle had been royal for the earlier part of its history and then became part of the Lancastrian inheritance which returned to the Crown when Henry IV ascended the throne. The conditions then were optimum for the survival of written records on the castle. The first reference is in 1179–80 in the Pipe Rolls (the annual financial statement by the sheriff of each county) where minor expenditure on works is recorded. The Pipe Rolls remain the main source until early in the next century when the Close and Patent Rolls furnish further information. From the later Middle Ages there is a wealth of Ministers' Accounts which, while not throwing much light on building operations, provides not a little information on the way life was led at the castle.

52 Pickering Castle, North Yorkshire: aerial view looking east.

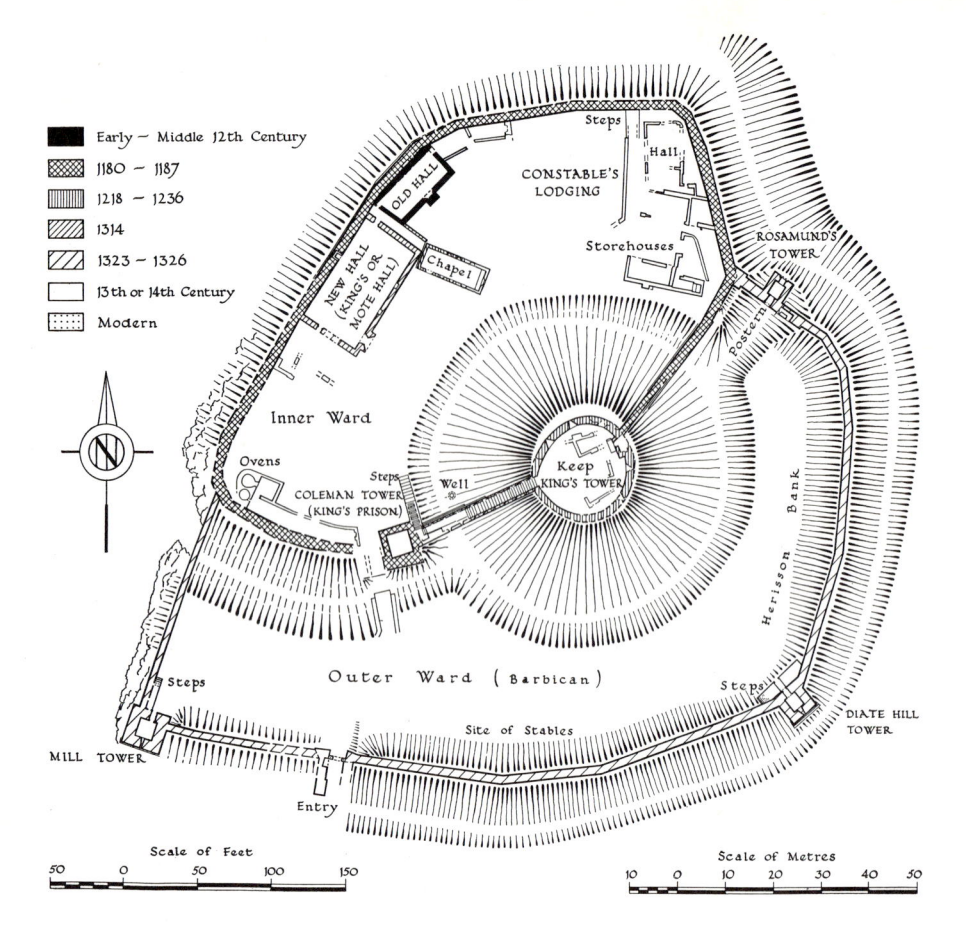

53 Pickering Castle, North Yorkshire: plan.

The castle is divided into two parts with the great motte between them (53). The motte is an earthen mound of made-up ground dug from the ditch and so could hardly have carried the weight of masonry on it now when it was first thrown up, nor indeed before a long period had elapsed for the soil to settle. From this it is reasonable to assume that the original castle was an earthwork of a design similar to the present one but with all the defences in wood, as this was the normal method of construction in the first hundred years after the Norman Conquest. To what date this earthwork castle at Pickering should be assigned cannot be decided with certainty; the author of the guide opted for the time of the Conqueror himself who came to Yorkshire on more than one occasion.

The masonry is clearly of more than one period, but how were the dates shown on the plan arrived at? After the execution of Thomas, Earl of Lancaster, in 1322 the castle came to the Crown for a short period; Edward II was there for three weeks in August, 1323 (mainly for hunting). On 10 August he gave a verbal instruction that the 'barbican' should be walled. From the nature of the work described in the instruction in the entry in the Close Roll there can be no doubt that the wall of the outer ward is meant, and it is known that the work was carried out. Most important of all the surviving curtain-wall with its square towers apart from the gatehouse is evidently of this period. Edward II was deposed and murdered in 1327, hence the dates of 1323–6 on the plan.

It is evident that the masonry of the inner ward is earlier. On the strength of its lancets the chapel (as well as the shell keep) has been assigned to early Henry III, but the curtain itself has been assigned to the Pipe Roll entries in Henry II's reign. There is record of a new hall being built in 1314; the architectural detail would allow us to regard the present remains only as part of a rebuild. Indeed greater precision has probably been given to the dating than is justified.

The second example is neither an abbey nor a castle but a large manor house of the later Middle Ages, its courtyards recalling Tudor houses rather than medieval castles. South Wingfield Manor in Derbyshire, near Alfreton, makes a bold silhouette on its hill that catches the attention of the approaching visitor. In spite of a modern farm being incorporated in it, the ruin is very impressive.

The visitor now enters through a hole in the south-west corner of the outer court, not by the original outer gatehouse in the south-east corner (54). The ranges are decidedly fragmentary in this outer court which is separated from the inner or northern court by a range with a gateway in the middle. At the west end of this range stand the fragmentary remains of the high tower, slighted after a Civil War siege. It is this fragment and the tall chimneys that give such a broken and striking form to the silhouette. The hall lies on the north side of the inner court on the right, over an undercroft, with the great presence-chamber over service rooms on the left, and kitchens at the far end. The west range consisted of lodgings of which only the external wall with its windows, fireplaces and latrines survives. The east range has vanished; the recovery of its plan by excavation should prove of great interest.

Apart from the insertion of a first floor into the hall after the Civil War, the whole of this massive ruin is clearly of one date, mid-fifteenth-century to judge by its abundant architectural detail. Furthermore, no one has doubted since its erection that the builder was Ralph, Lord Cromwell, who was also the builder of the great brick tower at his principal seat, Tattershall Castle, Lincolnshire (see p. 35). Among his papers that have survived in the possession of Viscount De Lisle is a building account covering the period 1 November 1442 to Christmas 1443 attached to the manorial account for that year.[7] The interpretation consisted in relating the account to the visible remains and vice versa. It would not be appropriate to enter into full details here, but some general points are well worth making.

Although the account covers a period of fourteen months, that was evidently only a fraction of the total time that must have been spent in construction. The first step, therefore, was to establish the point reached in the work and how long before it had started. At two points in the account there are references to three previous years, implying that this was the fourth accounting year. Counting backwards from 1 November 1442 the original contract could have been made in the autumn of 1439 or possibly the spring of 1440. Although there are references to an inner and outer court, the expenditure was devoted exclusively to the hall and west ranges of the inner court. From the nature of the work — plastering, erecting screens and louver,

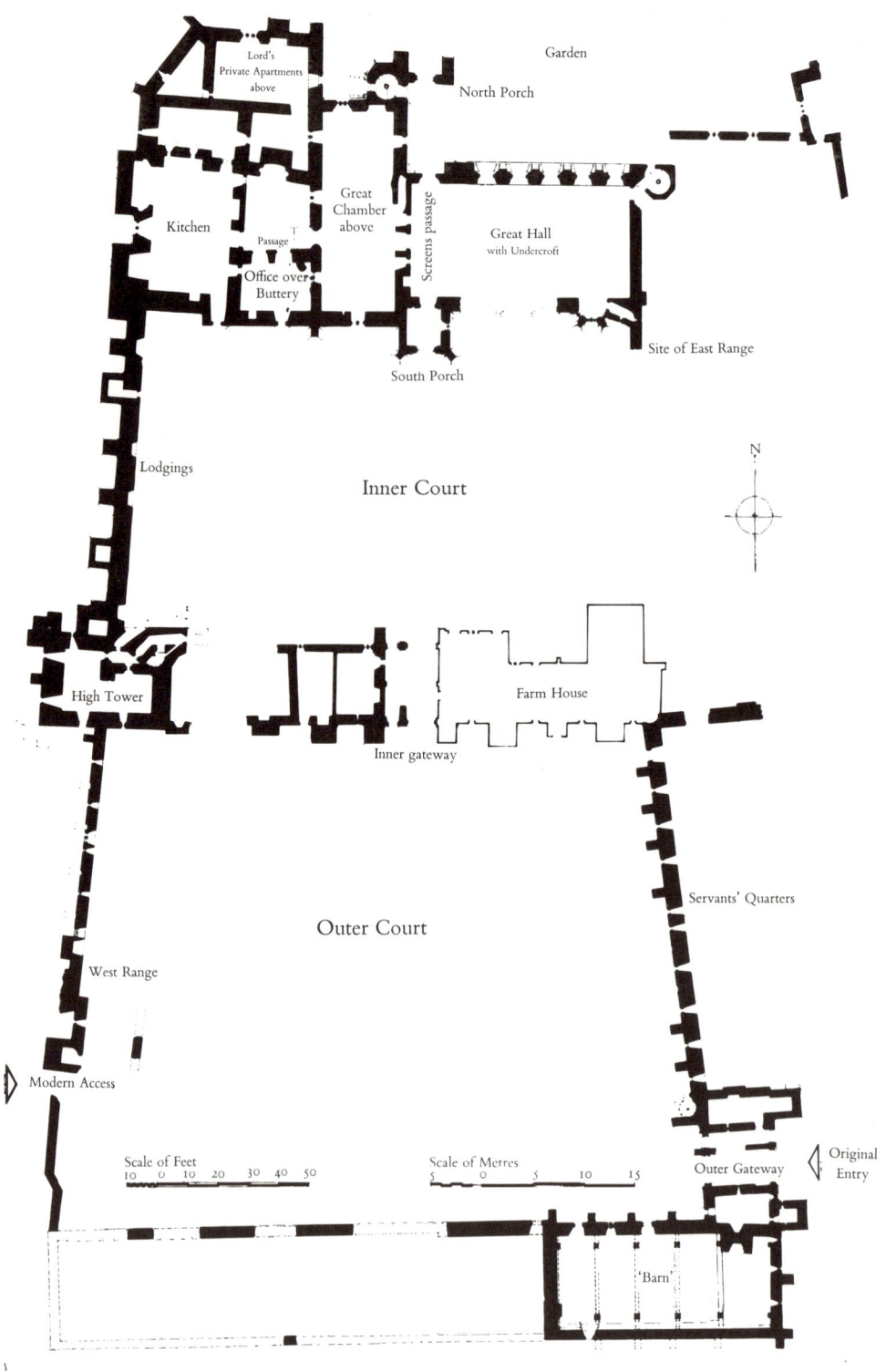

54 South Wingfield Manor, Derbyshire: plan of the ruin.

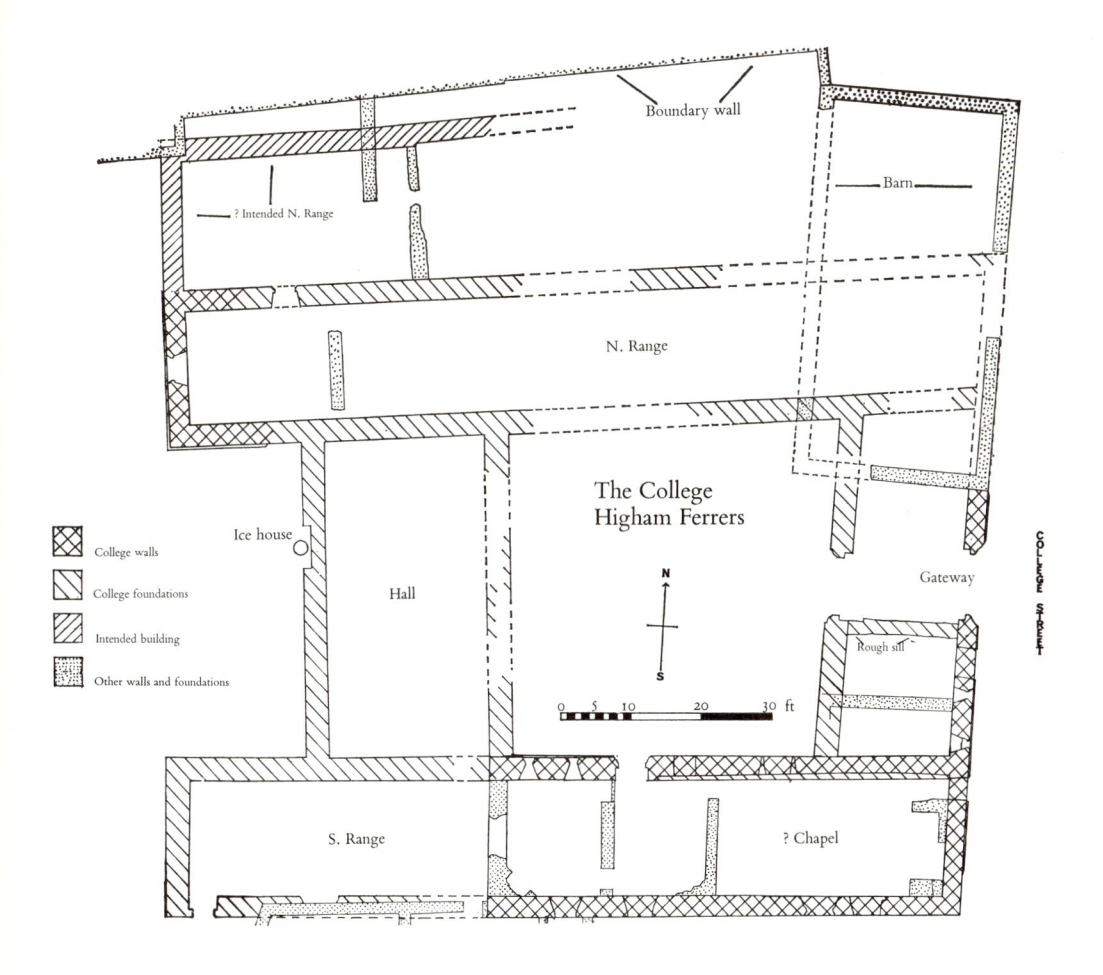

55 Higham Ferrers, Northamptonshire: plan of the college.

windows and so on—it is abundantly clear that this part of the inner court had reached completion. This is emphasised by the costs of cleaning up before the arrival of Lord Cromwell apparently to take up actual residence.

The sequence is therefore clear: work began in 1439–40 with the main design of courtyards laid out; the north and west ranges of the inner court were brought into use by the end of 1443; the other ranges, including the great tower, were constructed from 1444 to, say, 1452. Cromwell died in 1456 but he had already made provision in his will for the sale of Wingfield Manor (he had no children) to complete the college at Tattershall. It is likely, then, that he stopped work a few years before his death and we cannot even be certain that the manor was ever completed.

The interpretation can be carried further in the identification of rooms. For example, the parlour was in the missing east range on the first floor next to the hall, while the withdrawing chamber was north of the kitchen and entered from the great audience chamber. There is, in addition, a great mass of what could be described as information rather than interpretation, which includes the names of the workmen (Richard North being the leading mason), details of the louver, standard and vanes to be erected over the hall, ox-drawn wagons for transport, the building material and their place of origin, and so on. The interpretation of the account and the information it provides between them entirely alter the nature of this large but sad ruin.

In the third and last example the main task was an interpretation not of the written evidence but rather of an enigmatic plan.[8] Besides his well-known foundations at All Souls and St John's Colleges at Oxford, Archbishop Henry Chichele founded a modest chantry college at his birthplace, Higham Ferrers, a small town in Northamptonshire. The licence was received in 1422, and there is a fair amount of documentary evidence (a small cartulary survives) on this establishment for eight fellows, four clerks and six choristers. It was under-endowed, an important point in understanding its constructional development, and after the closure of the chantry colleges in Edward VI's reign, the buildings served variously as an inn and a farmyard. Since 1911 it has belonged to the Duchy of Lancaster who put it into the care of the Ministry of Works.

The plan (55) shows that the college consisted of a courtyard of rather mean ranges, 4.5 metres wide, of which the eastern part of the south range is still roofed, the rest being ruin or foundations. There is an interesting street frontage on the east. The interpretation required here was obviously an explanation of the evident alterations in plan, and the following was offered:

> 'The original intention may have been to form a courtyard, 115 feet square externally, on the street frontage with (following the Oxford pattern familiar to Chichele) three narrow lodgings ranges on west, south, and east and a broader range on the north to accommodate the hall and chapel. The south range, which is exactly the same length as the street frontage, was built first, perhaps for temporary accommodation and containing a chapel. Work began on the grander north range, but for some reason a drastic contraction in plan had to be made. As the college was under-endowed and chronically short of money the explanation for such a change may not be far to seek. The north range was now reduced to the standard 15 feet width and moved southward, while a new site was found for the hall in a broad west range brought forward to form a smaller courtyard. As the projection of the wings corresponds exactly to the width of a range, it is fair to presume that the west wall of the hall represents the east wall of the intended west range. There is no special provision for a chapel, although a chantry college without a place of worship is almost a contradiction in terms, and, indeed, we know from the documents that the founder intended a chapel and that the college had one throughout its life. Bridges, who saw the ruins early in the 18th century when much more survived than can be seen today, identified the existing roofed east end of the south range as the chapel by its fenestration ... If the suggestion is right that a proposed large north range was never built it must have been necessary to find an alternative place for the chapel by the conversion of a domestic range ...'[9]

This interpretation may have to be revised in the future but it renders intelligible the more perplexing features of the plan, clearly at this ruin the principal task confronting its would-be interpreter.

Conclusion

In a country like Italy where there is a profusion of Classical remains the Renaissance, which by definition was a rebirth of Classical studies, was bound to invest the remains of that period with particular interest and make them a source of admiration. In England where the Classical remains are either buried or unrecognisable this could not be so. The principal remains are monastic, reminders in a Protestant country of the Reformation, and so hardly the object of especial national affection and pride.[1] Neither is there in England that identification with Gothic architecture as a manifestation of the national genius that is found in France.[2] General de Gaulle urged his fellow countrymen to emulate the builders of the Gothic cathedrals.

In England the place held by ruins in the national consciousness is different from that held in France and Italy. One is tempted to say that from the point of view of ruins we belong to northern rather than Mediterranean Europe, although it is doubtful whether monastic ruins occur in such abundance in other Protestant parts of Europe. The abruptness of the end of the monasteries, the way it was done, the motives for the transference of the land—since the nineteenth century the gaunt ruins have tended to produce a feeling of unease.

The Picturesque, Romanticism, Revivalism, Morris and Arts and Carfts, archaeology —all have played their part and all exist today in influencing attitudes towards ruins. They were to some extent literary movements in origin, each not replacing but overlying what was there before. Romanticism was undoubtedly the most important since it vested the past with a significance and independence of its own but still with the vitality of the present, perhaps best exemplified in the novels of Sir Walter Scott. His imagination was fired by ruins about which the plot sometimes revolved as in *Kenilworth* or to a lesser extent in *Ivanhoe*. It is not a subject that needs to be pursued here since others have done it for us,[3] but it would be wrong to underestimate the influence of such novels on popular attitudes towards ruins. This genre continued in the nineteenth century, notably in the novels of W. H. Ainsworth, and as they were largely read by children, they implanted a veneration for ruins and ancient buildings at a very tender age, as well as an exaggerated notion of their evocative power.

The names of Gilbert Scott and Viollet-le-Duc have been coupled in this essay (see pp. 17–18), but there was one great difference between them: Scott numbered the Crown among his clients, but Viollet was the Inspecteur-Général, whose main restorations were for the French Government of Napoleon III. He recounts how the first Inspecteur-Général, just after his appointment in 1830, prepared a report for the Minister which included a recommendation on the total restoration of the great castle at Coucy.[4] Nothing happened, for as Viollet explained with some pride such a project was not realised until he took the restoration of Pierrefonds in hand. There was a sacramental character about his restoration; it was not a return to what had been before the structure became ruinous but an ideal not available to the medieval mason without the knowledge and technology of the nineteenth century. Indeed, the ideal cathedral or ideal castle was a preoccupation of the great Inspecteur-Général, as the drawings in his dictionary show.

It is inconceivable that in Victorian England the Government would have formally entered the field as in France, although the Crown did, of course, carry out restorations, for example, at the Tower of London. It might be argued that the controversies that raged about restoration in the final decades of the last century delayed Government intrusion into the preservation field; while it was uncertain as to how one ought to treat a ruin, it was wiser not to take sides. By the time there was full involvement the view of the Society for the Protection of Ancient Buildings generally prevailed—namely, that the object was to fix the ruin in the state in which it was found. This was not only cheaper than restoration but was also fairly easily carried out by a Government department.

To display only what is authentic must surely on moral, logical or economic grounds be the proper aim. Restoration in the last century was often prompted by the highest motives of piety and admiration for the Middle Ages, although usually with an innocent unawareness of the great chasm that separated the nineteenth century from the 'age of faith'. In the secular and mechanical world of today such illusions cannot be harboured. Restoration would now be repugnant, but an inflexible rule of retaining a ruin unaltered must pose a major dilemma for the preserver.

A building in use presents its roof to take the full brunt of the elements, but the laths and rafters, and the roof cover of tiles, slates or lead are regarded as periodically renewable. The eaves protect the outside face where again some renewal may be necessary. The interior is protected from the weather and, unless the wood is attacked by infection or infestation, should have an almost indefinite life. What a contrast to the ruin bared at all points to the elements and denied, as a matter of principle, the replacement of decayed stone. It may not fall down but it will gradually become unrecognisably worn. It would be a different story if there were some way of preserving the stone, but over the years a genuine stone preservative has proved as elusive as the alchemist's elixir for turning base metals into gold.

Leaving aside the impermanence of ruins, this essay has been concerned with their retrieval and display, in effect putting them to use rather than leaving them as picturesque but disintegrating masonry. The pleasure and satisfaction to be derived from a ruin are perhaps not as great as that experienced in a historic house and are certainly different in kind. The carpets, furniture and pictures are a distraction from the building itself, while in the ruin the harsh architectural reality is thrust upon us. The vicissitudes displayed in the ruin's history are perhaps a truer reflection of the brutal course of events over several generations than numerous portraits of figures in doublets and hose, wigs, top hats and tailcoats.

At first sight it might seem that the preservation of a ruin was not as complicated as that of a living building, and undoubtedly as far as physical treatment goes this is so. The range of materials required and their functional application in a structure in use creates a host of problems unknown in a ruin, if it is treated like a museum exhibit. The problems in a ruin are related to display rather than function and arise from centuries of degradation and neglect or from a use entirely different from that intended. It is largely a question of removing accumulations and intrusions of various kinds.

It might be said that, since technical problems of treatment within the province of the architect are only cursorily mentioned, this essay is mainly about the display of ruins. A large part of retrieval is consolidation of masonry, but examples have been chosen to illustrate the exposure of concealed remains for ultimate display. Display was the decisive consideration in much of the restoration mentioned, and 'representation', as the term is used here, is largely a display technique. Access and display are closely related, while the ultimate justification for the detailed interpretation described in Chapter 8 is to present a reliable and authoritative account of the ruin when it is on display. Indeed, the fact that the objective is to throw the ruin open to public view is bound to be an ever-present consideration in its treatment.

List of works referred to in abbreviated form

A	Antiquity	PRF	Roland Mortier, *La Poétique des ruines en France: ses origines, ses variations de la renaissance à Victor Hugo* (Histoire des idées et critique littéraire, vol. 144, Geneva, 1974)
AJ	*Archaeological Journal*		
HKW	H. M. Colvin (ed.), *The History of the King's Works*, vols i–ii (HMSO, 1963)		
MA	*Medieval Archaeology*		
NRAB	*Notes on the Repair of Ancient Buildings*, issued by the Society for the Protection of Ancient Buildings (London, 1903)	R	E. Viollet-le-Duc, *Dictionnaire raisonné de l'architecture française du xi-me au xvi-me siècle*, vol. viii (Paris, 1875), 'Restauration', 14–34
OG	*Official Guidebooks* (HMSO, since 1917). Annual list of current titles in *Sectional List, No. 17*	RIAM	*Report of the Inspector of Ancient Monuments for the year ending 31st March, 1913* (HMSO, 1913)
PPS	*Proceedings of the Prehistoric Society*		
PR	Rose Macaulay, *Pleasure of Ruins* (London, 1953)		

Notes

Introduction

1. As far as I know there is nothing published on reasons for differential survival among ruins. Other factors deleterious to buildings in use and ruins are wind and instability of foundations. Vegetation on ruins makes them even more vulnerable to wind, and instability of foundations clearly causes collapse in ruins; neither factor has a limited geographical distribution.
2. *PR*, 391.
3. All the earlier legislation has been repealed by the Ancient Monuments and Archaeological Areas Act 1979, but I am referring to the earlier Acts, particularly that of 1913.

PART I

1 Growth of Interest

1. W. S. Mackie (ed.), 'The Exeter Book, Part II', *Early English Text Society*, CXCIV (London, 1934), 198–9.
2. M. Aston, 'English Ruins and English History: the Dissolution and the Sense of the Past', *Journal of the Warburg and Courtauld Institute*, xxxvi (1973), 231–55. The analogy with the Revolution in France is very interesting: cf. Ch. XII in *PRF*.
3. Quoted by Aston, ibid., 251.
4. E. Thomas (ed.), *The Poems of John Dyer* (London, 1903), Grongar Hill, ll. 82–92.
5. William Gilpin, *Observations on the River Wye and Several Parts of South Wales, etc. relative chiefly to Picturesque Beauty* (London, 1782), 32–5. For the Picturesque generally see C. Hussey, *The Picturesque* (London, 1927).
6. Arthur Young, *A Six Months' Tour through the North of England . . .* (London, 1770), II, 322–5. This is very similar to the contemporary view of Diderot, *PRF*, 91.
7. Kenneth Woodbridge, *Landscape and Antiquity, Aspects of English Culture at Stourhead, 1718–1838* (Oxford, 1970), 168–70.
8. K. Clark, *The Gothic Revival* (London, 1950).
9. G. G. Scott, *Remarks on Secular and Domestic Architecture, Present and Future* (London, 1858), 116.
10. Sir G. G. Scott, *Lectures on the Rise and Development of Medieval Architecture Delivered at the Royal Academy* (London, 1879), i, 365.
11. At present in the Department of Art at the National Museum of Wales.
12. William Morris, *Architecture, Industry and Wealth: Collected Papers* (London, 1902), 200.
13. ibid., 204–5.
14. William Morris, *Architecture, History and Westminster Abbey* (London, 1900), 40.
15. *NRAB*, 12–13.
16. G. Baldwin Brown, *The Care of Ancient Monuments: An Account of Legislative and other Measures . . .* (Cambridge, 1905).
17. *RIAM*, 103. The two appendices, pp. 54–117, by the architect Mr Frank Baines, shed much light on the origin of contemporary practice.
18. M. W. Thompson, *General Pitt-Rivers, Evolution and Archaeology in the 19th Century* (Bradford on Avon, 1977).

2 Preservation

1. *RIAM*, 107–11. Cement was not used in 1913. Each mason tends to have his own recipe, varying the proportions slightly at will.
2. *MA*, IX (1965), 161–3. The extent of the destruction can be seen by the white on the plan marked as 'conjectural'.

3 Display

1. *HKW*.

PART II

4 Retrieval

1. M. W. Thompson, *Tattershall Castle, Lincolnshire* (National Trust, 1974), lists earlier works on the castle.
2. The collection of drawings has recently been reprinted: F. H. Reed, *Illustrations of Tattershall Castle ... 1872* (Harlequin Press, Sleaford, 1970).
3. C. R. Peers in *Antiquaries' Journal*, i (1921), 271–81; *AJ*, LXXXVI (1929), 20–8; OG (1933).
4. OG (1929) by C. R. Peers.
5. OG (1956) by O. E. Craster.
6. R. Gilyard-Beer, 'The Eastern Arm of the Abbey Church of Bury St Edmunds', *Proceedings of the Suffolk Institute of Archaeology*, XXXI (1970), 256–62.
7. A. B. Whittingham, 'Bury St Edmunds Abbey, The Plan, Design and Development of the Church and Monastic Buildings', *AJ*, CVIII (1951), 168–87.
8. M. W. Thompson, 'Recent Excavations in the Keep of Farnham Castle, Surrey', *MA*, IV (1960), 85–92; OG (1961) by M. W. Thompson.
9. M. W. Thompson, 'The Origins of Bolingbroke Castle, Lincolnshire', *MA*, X (1966), 152–8.
10. OG (1973) by J. D. K. Lloyd and J. K. Knight; *HKW*, 739–42.
11. OG pamphlet (1959) by M. W. Thompson.
12. OG (1965) by G. Webster.
13. P. Barker, 'Excavations on the Site of the Baths Basilica at Wroxeter', *Britannia*, VI (1975), 106–17.
14. P. R. Scott, *Guide to the Visible Remains of Roman Piercebridge* (Durham, 1977), 8–18.
15. J. Collingwood Bruce, *Handbook to the Roman Wall* (12th edn., ed. Sir Ian Richmond, 1966), 59–60.
16. *PPS*, XLIV (1978), 309–434.
17. *RIAM*, 15–16.

5 Restoration

1. *RIAM*, 4–10.
2. OG (1980) by A. J. Taylor.
3. OG (1917) by C. R. Peers; *RIAM*, 17–18.
4. A. Hamilton-Thompson, 'The Building Accounts of Kirby Muxloe Castle, 1480–1484', *Transactions of the Leicestershire Archaeological Society*, XI (1913–20), 193–345.
5. OG (1976) by M. W. Thompson.
6. OG (1978) by C. N. Johns.
7. OG (1947) by G. Chettle.
8. OG (1976) by M. W. Thompson.
9. Sir R. E. M. Wheeler, 'The Stanwick Fortifications, North Riding of Yorkshire', *Research Reports of the Society of Antiquaries*, XVII (London, 1954), 256–62.
10. *PPS*, XLIV (1978), 445.
11. R. J. C. Atkinson, 'Wayland's Smithy', *A*, XXXIX (1965), 125–33.
12. R. J. C. Atkinson, *Stonehenge* (London, 1956); *Stonehenge and Neighbouring Monuments* (HMSO, 1978).

6 Representation

1. *NRAB*, 34.
2. A. Keiller and S. Piggott, 'The Recent Excavations at Avebury', *A*, X (1936), 417–27; I. Smith, *Windmill Hill and Avebury, Excavations by Alexander Keiller, 1925–39* (Oxford, 1965), 175–224.
3. M. E. Cunnington, 'The "Sanctuary" on Overton Hill, near Avebury', *Wiltshire Archaeological and Natural History Magazine*, XLV (1932), 300–35.
4. M. E. Cunnington, *Woodhenge* (Devizes, 1929). The mass of concrete bollards has been irreverently called 'the tank trap', recalling as it does some of the defences of 1940!
5. S. Piggott, 'Timber Circles, A Re-examination', *AJ*, XCVI (1939), 193–222.
6. Rosemary Cramp, 'Excavations at the Saxon Monastic Sites of Wearmouth and Jarrow, Co. Durham: an Interim Report', *MA*, XIII (1969), 21–66.
7. OG (1965) by H. de S. Shortt.

7 Access

1. M. W. Thompson, 'Two Levels of the Mere at Kenilworth Castle, Warwickshire', *MA*, IX (1965), 156–61; OG (1976) by M. W. Thompson.
2. OG (1979) by A. J. Taylor.

8 Interpretation

1. The word is used in this sense in the title of *Ancient Monuments and their Interpretation, Essays Presented to A. J. Taylor*, M. R. Apted, R. Gilyard-Beer and A. D. Saunders (eds.), (Chichester, 1977).

2. *R*; nowhere has it been better expressed than by Viollet-le-Duc in his opening paragraphs.
3. Royal Commission on Historical Monuments, *An Inventory of the Historical Monuments in the City of Cambridge* (HMSO, 1959). The graph opposite p. lxxxiii seeks to correlate the amount of building at the colleges with the number of matriculations.
4. M. W. Thompson, 'The Date of Fox's Tower, Farnham Castle', *Surrey Archaeological Collections*, LVII (1960), 87–94.
5. *OG* (1958) by M. W. Thompson.
6. *HKW*, II, 780.
7. M. W. Thompson, 'The Construction of the Manor at South Wingfield, Derbyshire' in G. de G. Sieveking *et al.* (eds.), *Problems in Economic and Social Archaeology*, (London, 1976), 417–38.
8. M. W. Thompson, 'A Contraction in Plan at Archbishop Chichele's College in Higham Ferrers, Northants', *MA*, XI (1967), 255–7.
9. ibid., 257.

Conclusion

1. The situation may be contrasted with Ireland where monastic ruins are abundant but the sites are still venerated and used for burial by a Roman Catholic population.
2. In France ruins meant exclusively Classical ruins until the notion of Gothic ruins and follies was introduced from England in the second half of the eighteenth century; the Revolution, however, created a large number of genuine medieval ruins, and their preservation after 1815 became a major issue. There is, of course, a milder nationalistic element in England as well as in France. See *PRF*, Chs. XII and XV.
3. Hugh Honour, *Romanticism* (London, 1979), Chs. 4 and 5, especially 192 *et seq.* Ruins played an even more exaggerated part with Victor Hugo: Ch. XV in *PRF*.
4. *R*, 19–20.

Index

Page numbers in italic refer to illustrations.

Africa, North 9
Ainsworth, W. H. 95
All Souls College, Oxford 94
America, Central 9
Anglesey 22, 52
Asia Minor 9
Atkinson, Prof. R. J. C. 56, 65, 68
Aubrey, John 14
Avebury Circle, Wilts. 72

Barclodiad y Gawres tomb, Anglesey 54, 56
Bath 13
Bayon's Manor, Lincs. 12
beams, concrete 26, 52, 57, 72
Beaumaris Castle, Anglesey 58, *59*, 60, 84
Bede, Venerable 74
Beeston Castle, Ches. 32
Blundevill, Earl Randulph de 46
Bodiam Castle, Sussex 35, 58
Bolingbroke Castle, Lincs. 26, 43, 44, *45*, 46
bridges 30, 80, 82, 84
Brigantes, tribe of 64
Brown, G. Baldwin 20
Buck, S. and N., engravings by 15, *16*, 37, 46, 87
Burges, William, 7, 18, *19*, 35, 37, 63
Bury St Edmunds Abbey, Suffolk *26*, 27, 42
Bute, third Marquis of 7, 18, 58, 63; fourth Marquis of 63
Byland Abbey, Yorks. 37, *39*, 40

Caerleon, Roman fort, Gwent 50
Caernarfon Castle, Gwynedd 57, 58, 82, 88
Caernarfon town wall 33
Caerphilly Castle, Glam. *frontispiece*, *16*, 27, 35, *56*, 57, 58, 60, *62*, 63, *81*, 88
Cambridge University, colleges of 31
Camden, William 87
Carcassone 17, 18
Cardiff Castle, Glam. 7, 35, *36*, 63
Carn Euny, Cornwall, prehistoric village 54, 55, *70*, 72

cars, motor 10–11, 29–30, 77, 80
Castell Coch, Glam. 7, 18, *19*, 37, 63
Chichele, Archbishop Henry 94
Christ Church Cathedral, Canterbury 21
Christie, P. 54
Civil War 13, 14, 42, 46, 48, 63, 80, 91
Clare, Gilbert de, Lord of Glamorgan 60, 88
Close Rolls 89
Colchester town wall 13, 33
Conisbrough Castle, Yorks. 33, 47, 48, *81*, 82, 84, 88
concrete, use of 31–2
Conwy Castle, Gwynedd 83, 95
Cornwall 22, 54
Cramp, Professor Rosemary 74
Cromwell, Ralph, Lord 35, 91, 93
Cunnington, Mr and Mrs R. H. 72
Curzon, Lord 35, 37, 58

Dartmoor 52
de Gaulle, General Charles 95
De Lisle, Viscount 91
Denbigh town wall, Clwyd 33
Dere Street, Roman road 50
Din Lligwy, Anglesey, prehistoric village 52
Dissolution of the Monasteries 13, 14–15, 87
Dugdale, Sir William 14, 64, 80
Durham Cathedral 31, 40, 42
Dyer, John 15

Edward I 14, 32, 58, 82
Edward II 90, 91
Edward III 14
Edzell Castle, Angus 64
Elizabeth I 64, 80
Ely Cathedral 40
Environment, Department of 11

Farnham Castle, Surrey 42, 43, 44, 69, 88
fishponds 33
fogous 54, 71, 72
Fountains Abbey, N. Yorks. 15, 30, 33, 37, 77

102

gardens 63, 64
Gervase of Canterbury 87
Gibbon, Edward 18, 34
Gilpin, William 15
Gilyard-Beer, R. 7
Gloucester Cathedral 31
Goodrich Castle, Herefords. 37
Gothic Revival 18, 20
Grongar Hill, Dyfed 15
grouting 24

Hadrian's Wall 13, 50, 52, *53*, 64
Hamilton-Thompson, A. 14, 35
Harlech Castle, Gwynedd 32, *79*, 82
Hawley, Lt.-Col. W. 68
Helmsley Castle, N. Yorks. 84
Hereford town wall 33
Heddon-on-the-Wall, Northumb. 52, 53
Henry of Blois, Bishop of Winchester 42
Henry II 43
Henry IV 43, 89
Higham Ferrers, Northants, college at *93*, 94
Hoare, Sir Richard Colt 17
Holyhead, Anglesey 54
Hope, Sir William St John 21
hut circles 13, 52, 54

Indo-China 9

James of St George (d'Espéranches) 82

Jarrow monastery, Co. Durham 74, *74*
Johns, C. N. 63
Keiller, Alexander 72
Kenilworth Castle, War. 27, 30, 60, 63, 64, *78*, *79*, 80, 82
King's Works, History of the 87, 89
Kirby Hall, Northants 63
Kirby Muxloe Castle, Leics. 58, *61*, 88
Kirstall Abbey, Yorks. 33
Knight, J. K. 46

Lancaster, Duchy of 43, 89, 94
Leeds Castle, Kent 60
Leicester, Robert, Earl of 64, 80
Leland, John 80
Lincoln 13
Llanberis quarry workshops, Gwynedd 33
Llansteffan Castle, Dyfed *23*, 24
Llanthony Priory 17
Llewelyn ap Gruffud 63

Madoc's Rebellion 58
Menai Strait 58

Methodists 14
moats 33, 37, 44, 50, 60, 63
Montgomery Castle, Powys *45*, 46, *47*
Morris, William 18, 20, 33, 95
mortar 24, 48, 52, 71

Norwich town wall 33

Old Sarum 35, 75

Parc le Breos Cwm chambered tomb, Glam. *55*, 56
Patent Rolls 89
Peers, Sir Charles 21
Pembroke Castle 35
Peterborough Cathedral 40
Pickering Castle, N. Yorks. 89, *89*, 90, *90*, 91
Piercebridge Roman Fort, Co. Durham 50, *51*, 52
Pierrefonds, Chateau de 95
Piggott, Prof. S. 65, 68
Pipe Rolls 89
Pitt-Rivers, General A. H. L. F. 21
Plantagenet, Hamelin 48
portcullis grooves 82
Protection of Ancient Buildings, Society for the 18, 20, 71
Purbeck marble 10, 40

Reed, F. H. 37
Rievaulx Abbey, N. Yorks. 33, 37, *38*, 40, 75, 77
Rochester Castle keep, Kent 34
Roger, Bishop of Salisbury 75
Rome 15, 17
roofed buildings 28, 96
Royal Commission on Historic Monuments, Inventories of 87
Rufford Abbey, Notts. 27
Ruskin, John 20

St John's College, Oxford 74
St Joseph, Prof. J. K. 44, 46
Samarkand 9
sarsen stones 68, 72
Scott, Sir G. G. 18, 20, 95
Scott, Peter 50
Scott, Sir Walter 95
Shobdon Arches, Herefords. 17
Smith, C. 65
South Wingfield Manor, Derby. 91, *92*, *93*, 94
Stanwick Earthworks, N. Yorks. 22, 61, 64
Stephen, King 43

103

Stonehenge, Wilts. 22, 30, 52, 64, 65, *66*, 67, 68, 69
Stukeley, W. 72

tamping 52
Tattershall Castle, Lincs. 35, *36*, 37, 57, 58, 91
Tattershall College 91
Tees, river 50, 52
Thomas, Earl of Lancaster 90
tiled floors 40
Tintern Abbey, Gwent 37, 40, *41*, 75, 76, 77
Tower of London 96
Towey valley 15
Trefignath chambered tomb, Anglesey 65, 70, 71

vaults 28
Victoria County Histories 87, 89
Viollet-le-Duc, E. 17, 18, 95, 96
visitors to ruins 10, 29, 31, 32, 33, 34, 71

Wayland Smithy chambered tomb, Berks. 65, 66
Waynflete, Bishop William 42, 43
Weir, W. 35
Welsh Office 7, 63
Westminster Abbey 20
Wheeler, Sir R. E. M. 22, 64
Whitby Abbey, N. Yorks. 32
White Castle, Gwent *83*, 84
William I 90
Willis, Prof. Rev. Robert 21
Winchester Pipe Rolls 88
Woodhenge Circle, Wilts. 73, *73*
Works, Office of 11, 37, 71, 89
Wroxeter Roman town, Salop. 48, *49*, 50, 52, 73
Wye, river 15, 77

York 13
Young, Arthur 15